D1356076

THE LATE AUGUSTANS

THE POETRY BOOKSHELF

General Editor: James Reeves

Robert Graves: *English and Scottish Ballads*
Tom Scott: *Late Medieval Scots Poetry*
James Reeves: *Chaucer: Lyric and Allegory*
William Tydeman: *English Poetry 1400–1580*
Martin Seymour-Smith: *Shakespeare's Sonnets*
James Reeves: *John Donne*
Maurice Hussey: *Jonson and the Cavaliers*
Jack Dalglish: *Eight Metaphysical Poets*
James Reeves and Martin Seymour-Smith: *Andrew Marvell*
Dennis Burden: *Shorter Poems of John Milton*
V. de S. Pinto: *Poetry of the Restoration*
Roger Sharrock: *John Dryden*
James Reeves: *Jonathan Swift*
John Heath-Stubbs: *Alexander Pope*
Donald Davie: *The Late Augustans*
F. W. Bateson: *William Blake*
G. S. Fraser: *Robert Burns*
Roger Sharrock: *William Wordsworth*
James Reeves: *S. T. Coleridge*
Robin Skelton: *Lord Byron*
John Holloway: *P. B. Shelley*
James Reeves: *John Clare*
Robert Gittings: *Poems and Letters of John Keats*
Edmund Blunden: *Alfred Lord Tennyson*
James Reeves: *Robert Browning*
Denys Thompson: *Matthew Arnold*
James Reeves: *Emily Dickinson*
James Reeves: *G. M. Hopkins*
David Wright: *Seven Victorian Poets*
James Reeves: *The Modern Poets' World*
James Reeves: *D. H. Lawrence*
Martin Seymour-Smith: *Longer Elizabethan Poems*
James Reeves: *Geoffrey Chaucer*
Gareth Evans: *George Herbert*

ELEGY WRITTEN IN A COUNTRY CHURCHYARD
from a late eighteenth century engraving

THE LATE AUGUSTANS

1474047
821.08

LONGER POEMS OF THE
LATER EIGHTEENTH CENTURY

Edited with an Introduction
and Notes
by
DONALD DAVIE

HEINEMANN

LONDON

Heinemann Educational Books Ltd
LONDON   MELBOURNE   TORONTO
SINGAPORE   JOHANNESBURG
HONG KONG   NAIROBI
AUCKLAND   IBADAN
NEW DELHI

© DONALD DAVIE 1958

ISBN 0 435 15018 9 (cased edition)
435 15019 7 (paperback)

FIRST PUBLISHED 1958
REPRINTED 1963, 1965, 1968, 1971

Published by
Heinemann Educational Books Ltd
48 Charles Street, London W1X 8AH
Printed in Great Britain by Morrison and Gibb Ltd
London and Edinburgh

CONTENTS

ACKNOWLEDGMENTS

For help in preparing this anthology I am grateful to Charles Tomlinson, and to my colleagues, David Large and F. S. L. Lyons of Dublin University, and Professor Joseph Foladare of Santa Barbara College in the University of California. I am more particularly indebted to Mr. F. W. Bateson, who read the typescript of the whole and pointed out several errors. Those which remain are due to my perversity, not to his oversight.

D. D.

NOTE TO THE SECOND EDITION

For this edition I have altered the punctuation throughout Smart's *A Song to David* in accordance with modern usage. I have profited in this respect from the edition of the poem by J. B. Broadbent (Rampant Lions Press 1960).

D. D.

INTRODUCTION

OF the poems in this anthology, the earliest is Shenstone's *The School-Mistress*, written between 1737 and 1748, and the latest is Wordsworth's *Old Cumberland Beggar*, written 1797–98. In between come Johnson's *Vanity of Human Wishes*, published in 1749; Gray's *Elegy*, in 1750; Smart's *A Song to David* in 1763; Goldsmith's *Deserted Village* (1770), and his *Retaliation*, published after his death in 1774; then, *The Country Justice*, by Langhorne, published in three parts in 1774, 1775, and 1777; and finally Cowper's *Yardley-Oak*, written in 1791.

Thus the collection covers a span of roughly sixty years, from 1740 to the end of the eighteenth century; and we must not suppose that Shenstone and Cowper were contemporaries, that Shenstone's world was the same as Cowper's. Wordsworth indeed is most often thought of as the voice of a new age. But there is still a very general assumption that the clocks of literary history stopped, if not in 1700, then at the death of Pope in 1744; and that they began to tick again only in 1798, when Wordsworth and Coleridge published their *Lyrical Ballads*.

(1) POLITICS AND MORALE. If this is true, if poetry is at a stand-still in this period, then it must be fatally out of touch with an age which saw rapid and far-reaching changes in all other fields. 'Complacency', we are often told, is an attitude character-istic of the whole of this period. Yet in the 1740s, writes Professor Louis Bredvold, 'Poets and satirists alike show the age involved in darkness'. In 1740 Sir Robert Walpole was still at the head of affairs, a minister who (to quote Professor Bredvold again) 'enjoys a bad pre-eminence among English statesmen for drawing upon himself the hostility of writers of all parties and shades of party, men representing the best elements in the

nation'. Long after Walpole had left the political scene, it was common form among writers to cry out with William Pitt the elder on 'this gloomy scene' and 'this disgraced country'. As late as 1757 John Brown enjoyed a great success with his 'Estimate of the Manners and Principles of the Times', in which he accused his contemporaries of 'a vain, luxurious, and selfish effeminacy'. The change of key came with the unprecedented successes of the Seven Years War (1756–63), when the same William Pitt, Earl of Chatham, acting through Wolfe in Canada, Clive in India, Boscawen and Hawke on the high seas, decisively outdistanced the old rival France in the race for overseas possessions and colonial trade. Undoubtedly this gave a great fillip to national morale, so that Dr. Johnson, who in his early satire, 'London', had been among the most pessimistic critics of England under Walpole, could indulge in his better-known later prose writings an assurance in the political good sense of English conservatism which we have some right to describe as 'complacent'. Yet by 1776 the successful insurrection of the American colonists was once again raising the direst forebodings in the minds of thinking men, and our period ends with the panicky measures of the younger Pitt, suppressing any expressions of sympathy with the French Revolution, employing spies and paid informers, continually retrenching civil liberties.

(2) INDUSTRY AND SOCIETY. These changes in public opinion and sentiment on political affairs were largely a confused reflection of far-reaching changes in the social structure and the national economy. One of the most striking of these changes was the increased importance of unskilled labour. By 1790 there was already an urgent need of factory hands, to work in the new urban factories made possible by technical inventions such as the spindled spinning jenny of James Hargreaves and the spinning frame of Richard Arkwright, both perfected in the 1760s. When Samuel Crompton in 1779 combined the two in a machine not different in principle from the spinning

machines of today, the British cotton industry was born, and in the early years of the nineteenth century became as important to the national economy as the wool-producing and wool-working which had been for centuries the basis of Britain's prosperity. That, too, had been an industry, but an industry without factories, employing men who were often their own masters and in any case skilled craftsmen in their own right; the change is gradual over the eighteenth century, from the craftsman working in his home, sometimes buying his own raw materials and even owning his own appliances, to the relatively unskilled factory-hand. Other industries, such as iron-smelting and the mining of coal, had to expand in order to produce the machinery and the fuel which the factories required; and this expansion was accomplished in a similar way, by consolidating numbers of small enterprises in larger concerns which could afford new machines—the steam-pump, for instance, in the case of mining—which were invented to meet just this need for increased production.

All these changes, which with many others we now group under the heading of the Industrial Revolution, go unremarked in literature until the nineteenth century is far advanced. And it may well be objected that the absence of any reference to these matters gives a certain air of unreality to the literature of our period, as of the period which follows it. But it's important to realise that the poets, for instance, did not deliberately close their eyes to what was going on under their noses. Still less, if they had noticed it, would they have excluded it from their poetry as essentially 'unpoetic'; on the contrary, this is a period when many poets believe that no subjects are outside the scope of poetry if only the poet is skilful enough—it is the period when William Falconer, in *The Shipwreck*, treated in verse of the science of marine navigation, and when Erasmus Darwin in his *Loves of the Plants* versified the science of botany. The truth is more extraordinary: these vast changes went unnoticed by a large part of the nation. The politicians themselves were unaware of them. They were known only to a few men like Richard Arkwright who was not only an inspired technician but also a financier, truly a captain of industry; to a few men like Arkwright and, as a fact of experience which they could not comprehend, to the inarticulate mass of the peasantry who found themselves starved out of their villages and herded to the towns.

(3) THE AGRARIAN BACKGROUND. And this was precisely the aspect of the matter which was apparent to the poets. Typically, the poet of the period was a country gentleman like Shenstone and Cowper, or a country clergyman like Langhorne and George Crabbe. So we get the paradox that in literature the Industrial Revolution is recorded almost exclusively in its effect upon agrarian England. The poets saw what was happening to rural England without understanding why it was happening. And, indeed, it wasn't easy to see. One reason for destitution in the rural areas was quite simply a great increase in population; and it was hardly the needs of industry that impelled the English to breed faster. Yet the result was, as Dr. Bronowski notes in his study of Blake, that in Blake's lifetime England ceased to grow anything like enough corn to feed herself. As a result the price of bread soared; and though this meant that the producer got a better price for his corn, this helped only the fairly big farmer, not the independent smallholder. For in agriculture as in industry, measures for increased efficiency paradoxically spelt disaster for all but the big operators. There was an agricultural revolution alongside the industrial one; but many of the advances in agricultural technique required, to be exploited properly, an estate or a large farm. Thus the most enlightened cultivators joined hands with the plutocratic 'Nabobs' execrated by Langhorne and Goldsmith, who invested in landed estates in England the fortunes they had made in the East or West Indies; for different reasons both sorts of land-owner wanted to buy out the independent smallholder, take over the land farmed by their tenants, and enclose the commons.

Since mediaeval times each English village had reserved tracts of land to be the common property of all the villagers; and for the peasant villager the rights of grazing his cattle and cutting fuel on this common land could make all the difference between subsistence and penury. As in the sixteenth century a boom in the wool industry had caused commons to be enclosed for sheep-walks, so now enclosure of the commons began again, this time for the growing of grain, or else for the 'landscaping' of some adjoining estate.[1] Yet the enclosure of common land was normally less important than the other sort of enclosure which was designed simply to re-allot in workable units the privately owned strips in the erstwhile 'open' fields. And the chief cause of rural distress was the rise in rural population, which arose from the relative prosperity of the village in the first half of the eighteenth century, when better housing and sanitation forced up the birthrate. These processes, with the vagrancy and destitution which they occasioned, and the inadequacy of the Poor Laws to deal with them, are in the background of Goldsmith's *Deserted Village* and Langhorne's *Country Justice* no less than Wordsworth's *Old Cumberland Beggar*.

(4) PROVINCIALISM. Moreover, the belief that what was being destroyed was a sturdy simplicity worth more than urban knowingness—this was no novel idea introduced by Wordsworth. Long before 1798, and even before the British intellectuals felt the impact of Rousseau, there was a high premium placed on artless simplicity, and an attempt to find it in the child and the nobly untutored savage no less than in the humble son of the soil. It may be suspected, however, that these ideas made most appeal to those who were themselves furthest from innocence; and it was the world-wearied sophisticates of the

---

[1] The vogue for landscape-gardening (of which an early showpiece, though on a small scale, was Shenstone's estate, the Leasowes) was something more than a fad. It rested upon the true and arresting idea that the park of a country house should make an aesthetic transition between the untidy beauty of the countryside and the ordered elegance of the house's architecture.

metropolis who rushed to pay their respects to barbarian chieftains,[1] just as it was they who patronized milk-woman poetesses and thresher-poets like Stephen Duck. The hectic instability of metropolitan life, ruled by fad and sensationalism, was censured by Wordsworth in a famous passage of his preface to *Lyrical Ballads*; but in this too he had been anticipated by Shenstone and Cowper, just as his own supposedly quite unromantic contemporaries, Jane Austen and George Crabbe, were at one with him in valuing provincial life above metropolitan. Indeed, nothing is so remarkable about our period as the steady alienation of the serious artist from London. In Pope's lifetime to have to live anywhere but in the capital, or within easy reach of it, was taken to be a sentence of banishment; yet in the next two or three generations the serious writer who lived in London was rather the exception than the rule. The glaring exception, who not only lived in London but for whom to live elsewhere was unthinkable, is Johnson, in this as in much else (in his critical principles, for instance, and his poetic style) an untypical conservative, harking back to the age of Pope and Queen Anne.

And indeed London, though it was the commercial and political capital, was not the place to listen for the beating of the nation's heart. That was to be heard in Manchester and industrial Shropshire on the one hand (where no poet was there to listen), or else in the ravaged villages of the agrarian south, their people drifting off the land towards the cotton mills of Manchester, the foundries of Ironbridge, or Josiah Wedgwood's Staffordshire potteries. London, at neither the losing nor the receiving end, was perhaps the worst vantage-point.

The move to the provinces—more often, the willingness to

[1] In 1772, Captain Cartwright, explorer of Labrador, brought home a family of five Esquimaux, who were presented at Court, and were a nine days' wonder to fashionable London. In 1773 Omai, a South Sea islander brought home by Captain Furneaux after Cook's second voyage to the Pacific, enjoyed an even greater success and was portrayed by Reynolds.

stay there—is related to a new liveliness and civility in many of the provincial centres. This is the period when the Assembly Rooms are built in many provincial cities; and for thirty years, off and on (1731–62), the city of York, for instance, seems to have provided the novelist Laurence Sterne with as much as he needed of civilised society and cultural amenities. What is true of English provincial cities holds still truer of Edinburgh and Dublin, capitals in their own right. This is the great age of urban culture in both these cities, as appears from their architecture. Had Swift lived fifty years later, he could no longer have felt so exiled by his appointment to St. Patrick's; for the Dublin of Grattan's parliament, of the architecture of Gandon and the patronage of Lord Charlemont, of the oratory of Curran and Flood, was a true metropolis, truly a European capital. Yet the most talented Irishmen—Burke, Sheridan, Goldsmith—still very often sought their fortunes in London; whereas in the 1760s and 1770s Edinburgh, as 'the Athens of the North', contrived to keep many of her most illustrious sons—David Hume and Adam Smith for instance—at home.

(5) PRE-ROMANTICISM AND THE SCOTTISH INFLUENCE. The Scottish contribution to English literature in this period, and indeed to the literature and thought of Europe, is astonishingly extensive. Burns and Boswell, Hume and Adam Smith were men of genius; but it is almost more important to notice some exceptionally influential works by relatively undistinguished minds. Henry Mackenzie's *Man of Feeling*, for instance, which came out in 1771, by diluting and simplifying the *données* of Sterne and Richardson and, more remotely, of Rousseau, has a good claim to be the ancestor of what we know now as the middle-brow best-seller; and by the end of the century there was, as most people know from Jane Austen's *Northanger Abbey*, a middle-brow public which has grown in size and importance ever since.

This public, feeding upon just such a skilful adulteration as

Mackenzie first effected, is largely female. For one of the momentous developments in English society of the late eighteenth century is the emancipation of the middle-class Englishwoman, who partly profited by, partly herself brought about, the striking refinement of middle-class manners which we perceive in the contrast between the hard-drinking masculine society of Henry Fielding's country gentry and the drawing-rooms of a novel by Fanny Burney or Jane Austen. Accordingly, if the middle-class Englishwoman, now educated like her brother though by no means so extensively, demanded the sort of sub-literature represented by the so-called 'Tale of Terror', we should also remember with respect the many women of the period who, not content with stopping short of their brothers, strenuously educated themselves. From about 1760 onwards is the great age of the blue-stocking. Often witty and charming as well as knowledgeable and formidably serious, 'the blues' were women who dedicated themselves, with worthwhile effectiveness, to the task of civilising and refining society, by insisting that woman's status be acknowledged. Sheridan's Mrs. Malaprop is an example of such a woman at an early stage in her course of self-improvement when she still makes comic blunders.

Mackenzie, however, when he implied in his novel, indeed in its very title, that the true mark of distinction in humankind was not sound judgment but rather emotional susceptibility, less a clear head than a tender heart, appealed to much more than just the new reading public of bourgeois women. Just as it was the very artful society of the metropolis which responded to the appeal of the artless, so we may suppose it was only the unfeeling and sophisticated who recognized anything problematical in the necessity for 'feeling'. And so the 'feelings' they sought and plumed themselves on possessing are of a specially complicated and ambiguous sort, as if their jaded palates demanded ever more curious combinations of emotional ingredients in order to taste at all. John Logan, a very minor

poetaster and again a Scot, catches the flavour of this sentiment-
ality when he writes:

> Nor will I court Lethean streams,
> The sorrowing sense to steep;
> Nor drink oblivion of the themes
> On which I love to weep.

It is plainly an enervated sensibility which will sympathize with
the poet who doesn't want to forget his sorrow just because he
is enjoying it. To the historian of culture, the period 1740 to
1800 in England appears under the two aspects of an Augustan
decadence and a pre-Romantic false dawn. It is difficult to give
full weight to both these aspects in the case of any given writer
or given work; it is still more difficult to realise that the age is
often at its most decadent when it seems most clearly to look
forward towards Romanticism, as in this emphasis on 'feeling'.

A yet more striking example of a second-rate Scottish mind
seizing upon the need of the time and becoming influential all
over Europe is afforded by the career of James Macpherson,
the famous 'Ossian', who in his prose-poems *Fragments of
Ancient Poetry* (1760), *Fingal* (1761), and *Temora* (1763), claimed
to be translating from the Gaelic of the Scottish Highlands.
The imposition deceived all Europe and was not dispelled
until after Macpherson's so-called sources were printed in the
Gaelic in 1807. And yet Macpherson cannot be called simply a
literary forger, for the ethics of scholarship were much less
rigid in his day than in ours. If Macpherson trimmed and
expanded and adapted his material out of all recognition, and
to the extent that 'translation' is certainly a misnomer for his
pieces of poetic prose, yet this differs only in degree from the
practice of Bishop Percy in his *Reliques of Ancient English
Poetry*, which is accounted a piece of respectable and indeed
epoch-making scholarship. For Percy no less than Macpherson
took it for granted that his English ballads had to be tampered
with extensively before they could be presented to the public.
Even Thomas Chatterton, the boy prodigy of Bristol, who had

no 'originals' at all for the poems he attributed to a fifteenth-century poet Rowley, can hardly be put down as a simple forger; for we perceive that in these imitations (Spenserian in substance, though made to seem older by arbitrary archaisms of spelling), he occasionally attains to a force and freshness notably absent from the poems he wrote in the style and language of his own time. It is as if the boy lived more truly and fully in the imaginary character he had made for himself, than in his own person. And there is a similar dubiety about several of the quite numerous charlatans and self-deluders of the time. What is more important is to note how the motive behind these writers must also have operated in the readers they deluded; and this motive cannot be other than a widespread dissatisfaction with the culture of their own time, or at any rate with the would-be exclusive claims of that culture, and a hazy conviction that cultural riches lay hidden in ages other than the Roman age of Augustus and those one or two other peak-periods which the true Augustan (hence the name) laid down as alone worthy of study and imitation. Quite plainly, however far from scientific strictness in their operations, the Macphersons and Percies and their readers are the ancestors of the scientific anthropologists and archaeologists of today.

THE POETS

ROBERT BURNS, by any account the greatest Scottish poet of this time, may seem conspicuous by his absence from this collection. But to call Burns a Scottish poet does not mean just that he was a poet and a Scotsman, but that his true significance —historically speaking—can be realised only when he is seen in the perspective of a cultural tradition quite distinct from the English. It has been truly remarked, for instance, that Burns's satires can be appreciated as such only when we recall the Renaissance connection between 'satire' and 'satyr'; the savage elation of *Tam o' Shanter* seems to express the Bacchanalian energy with which morally repressed communities, like those of the Scottish Calvinist villages, seized on the rare occasions of permitted licence and self-expression. Read in conjunction with the satires of Johnson or Churchill, *Tam o' Shanter* can only cloud our understanding of those poems and lose significance itself. It has nothing to do with them, nor with Pope and Dryden, Horace and Juvenal, who stand behind them; its place is with the flytings and macabre humour of the great Scottish poets of the late Middle Ages. Of Burns's exquisite songs much the same needs to be said; as Mr. W. A. Edwards has rightly pointed out, in most of these too we have to hear the hobnails beating out the time of strathspey or reel. Because the literary historians have treated Burns as an English dialect poet, they have applauded him as the earliest poet of the true Romantic movement (his *Poems, Chiefly in the Scottish Dialect*, appeared in 1786); but in fact, just because Burns was a Scottish poet, the whole notion of 'a Romantic movement', as applied to English poetry, is irrelevant, a needless confusion. And yet the strongest case for the inclusion of Burns would rest upon just this recognition, that Burns was adopted into the English tradition as it were posthumously; for, before the literary historians, it was the poet Wordsworth who regarded Burns as the harbinger and pioneer of the Romantic lyrics Wordsworth himself was writing, and thus though Burns was not an English Romantic while he lived or when he died, yet in a sense he had become an English Romantic by the time of the death of Wordsworth.[1]

A better case could be made for one of Burns's countrymen, of by no means comparable genius but still a formidable talent, JAMES THOMSON. A Scot and a true poet, Thomson is not at all a Scottish poet in the same sense as Burns. It is plain that he regarded himself as contributing not to the Scottish tradition but to the English one; and his contribution is considerable. In particular, as he was one of the first, so he was certainly the

[1] Byron, for instance, in a romantic satire like *The Vision of Judgement*, is in spirit as near to Burns the satirist as to Pope.

most successful of the many poets who tried in the eighteenth century to incorporate into the English tradition, as part of the technical repertoire each subsequent poet can draw upon, the procedures of Milton's blank verse. The twentieth century, in the figures of Mr. T. S. Eliot and Mr. Ezra Pound, has given added corroboration to what is one of the most curious and most conclusively documented features of the English poetic tradition—the way in which Milton's use of the language refuses to be incorporated in this way, remaining eccentric and peculiar to Milton himself. Thomson alone in his *Seasons* (first written in the 1720s but continually revised up to 1744) contrived to imitate Milton's latinate vocabulary and syntax, while retaining a tone of voice distinctly his own. Partly this success was due to his finding a limited but valuable subject-matter which was entirely unMiltonic, the appearance of the countryside changing as the seasons change. This is now so familiar as a subject for poetry that it is hard to realise what a novelty it was for Thomson's first readers to have this presented as self-sufficient matter for poems. Doubtless they were led to see it freshly in this way because, like Thomson himself, or else with Thomson's assistance, their view of seasonal change (and particularly of the atmospheric effect of different kinds of weather) was informed on the one hand by the discoveries of landscape-painters, on the other by the speculations of Sir Isaac Newton in his *Opticks*, and of other scientists, on the nature of light and the processes of human vision. Thomson also wrote poems of political exhortation such as *Liberty* (1736), and a Spenserian poem, *The Castle of Indolence*. He died in 1748.

In speaking of Milton's influence it is necessary to distinguish between the blank verse of the Miltonic epics on the one hand, and Milton's earlier lyrical poems, including the blank verse, *Comus*. Where the mature blank verse resisted any attempt at fruitful imitation, poems such as *Lycidas* and *Il Penseroso* were drawn upon constantly and successfully—never to better effect than by WILLIAM COLLINS. One of the most conscious and meticulous of poets, Collins wrote very few poems, in all of which the slender and fugitive feeling is coaxed into expression through a delicate manipulation of the devices of previous poetry, Greek and Roman on the one hand, English on the other. As for the pre-eminence of Milton among the English models, Collins's metrical forms in themselves are telling evidence.[1] And as regards the Miltonic element in the diction, where it is just as pervasive and rather more important, it is sufficient to refer to Dr. F. R. Leavis's analysis, in his *Revaluation*, of the debts to *Lycidas* in Collins's finest poem, the *Ode to Evening*. But others of Collins's English predecessors are drawn upon, notably Thomson, whom he honoured in a moving poem after his death. Like Thomson and the painter-poet JOHN DYER, author of the famous *Grongar Hill* (1726), Collins exploits the discoveries of the landscape-painters, especially their calculated indistinctness; and like Thomson again he elaborates the poetic personification into an allegorical set-piece. His allegiance to the earlier Milton rather than the later allies him less with Thomson than with JOSEPH WARTON (1722–1800), who, like his brother THOMAS (1728–90), tried, by re-writing the history of English poetry, to liberate the poet's imagination from the rational confines built around it (as they thought) by Pope and Pope's admirers. It is significant that one can write of Collins most easily in terms of tendencies floating in the air of his period and shared by others, which only he was able with exquisite tact to combine into precarious synthesis.

EDWARD YOUNG, though he was born as early as 1683, did not publish his most famous and influential work, *Night Thoughts on Life, Death and Immortality*, until the 1740s. As with Thomson, so with Young, it is not easy to determine whether his true affinity is with the age of Pope, or with the succeeding age. As Thomson is certainly of a later age than Pope in the attention he pays to scenery, so the heavily contrived gloom which broods over *Night Thoughts* is obviously

[1] See John Butt, *The Augustan Age*, pp. 96–100.

related, through Robert Blair's *The Grave* of 1743 and James Hervey's prose *Meditations among the Tombs* (1745–7), to the exquisitely savoured melancholy of the sensibility-cult at the end of the century. On the other hand, while Young's blank verse is certainly tinged by the Miltonic elements more thoroughly mastered by Thomson, it also shows—and far more plainly—a consistent reaching after the point and memorability of Pope, being terse and exclamatory, its unit much less the verse-paragraph than the packed aphorism.

Spenser's influence can be detected in Dryden and Pope, and in poets such as Johnson later in the century, whom we do not think of as Spenserians. The latter, laborious imitators of Spenser's stanza and his diction, are chiefly memorable for the many words lost to the language between Spenser's day and theirs, which they restored to currency.[1] Only three of the many Spenserian imitations can claim intrinsic importance over and above their historical significance. These are Thomson's *Castle of Indolence*, Shenstone's *School-Mistress*, and (a good deal less certainly) *The Minstrel* (1771–4) of the Scot, James Beattie. *The School-Mistress* is chosen here to represent this kind of poem because the aspect of Spenser which attracts Shenstone, and which he tries to reproduce, is Spenser's humane feeling, an element less obvious than what appealed to Thomson or to Beattie, and in the last resort more important.

WILLIAM SHENSTONE (1714–63) is undoubtedly very small beer as a poet, yet attractive and even admirable as a person. Apart from *The School-Mistress*, his most interesting poems are the 'Elegies'; and of these only the one that appears in the *Oxford Book of Eighteenth-Century Verse* is wholly successful and memorable. The Elegies seem, at first sight, just a mellifluous rendering of the moral commonplaces of Shenstone's generation. One should, he seems to say, despise the pursuit of fame

[1] Professor Butt gives the following striking examples: 'aghast', 'appal', 'avail', 'carol', 'dreary', 'forlorn', 'glee', 'guerdon', 'miscreant', 'poignant', 'ribauld', 'uncouth', 'welkin'.

in favour of the rural seclusion of his country seat, where, in friendship and 'chearful' society, temperance and candour may flourish as they cannot in the court or the town.[1] And the passions must be controlled by rational good sense. We agree, but yawning. For we miss in Shenstone the tension and pressure which give force to much the same morality when we find it in Pope or Johnson. To maintain these standards in the face of profound misanthropy or misfortune or a gnawing sense of guilt—this is heroic; to a man of such low vitality as Shenstone they seem to come altogether too easily. And yet we must honour him for honestly admitting as much:

> Ere reason learns by study'd laws to reign,
> The weaken'd passions, self-subdued, obey.

His difficulty was not in governing or subduing the fires, but in keeping the wraith of feeling alight.

This is even truer of the poets who reject this conservative morality, and the poetic procedures which go with it, than of those, like Shenstone, who adhere to them. To many critics it has seemed that the Augustan order, in moral conduct and in art, was thrown down by individuals who experienced surges of feeling too powerful to be accommodated in the Augustan system. This version of the change hardly squares with the facts. THOMAS GRAY, for instance, having wrought to consummate perfection, in his *Elegy Written in a Country Churchyard*, the trains of thought and feeling, the diction and the metrical forms that we find in Shenstone's elegies, after 1750 grew thoroughly discontented with his own achievement, and strove, in Pindaric Odes and imitations from Old Welsh and Old Norse, to give English poetry a new infusion of impetuous if barbaric energy, and unbridled passion. Yet this poet, applauded by Beattie and others for striking out so boldly, was in fact a timorous

[1] 'Chearfulness' and 'candour' are key-notions in the eighteenth century, and have changed in meaning confusingly since then. See, on 'candour', William Empson's *Structure of Complex Words*.

valetudinarian. Even in secluded Cambridge (though for that matter Cambridge life may have aggravated the propensity), it appears that life was too hectic for Gray to endure. In fact, like Shenstone (and like Collins, whose nervous depression amounted at times to insanity), Gray seems to have been distinguished by low vitality. One comes to think, indeed, that it was enervation, not energy, which fretted most under the Augustan dispensation. The Augustan chains were chafed away; they were not broken. It was harder to be Augustan if you did not feel enough, than if you felt too much.

It is no accident, for instance, that the most impregnably Augustan of all the poets of this age is the one who survives as the most massive and forceful personality. Boswell can be misleading, not only because he paints an elderly Johnson secure in status and prestige, whereas the younger SAMUEL JOHNSON who wrote *The Vanity of Human Wishes* was struggling in want as a hack-journalist; but also because he has created the impression that the unique prestige of the older Johnson came about because in his opinions and attitudes he represented the consensus of opinion at the time. From this misapprehension it is a short step to seeing in Johnson a TV personality born before his time, his calculated rudeness permitted and applauded because he was 'the common man' writ large, voicing the clubman's hearty commonsense. In fact, a very slight knowledge of the currents of literary opinion in Johnson's England will show that, far from voicing opinions commonly held, Johnson represented rather a stubborn rearguard, holding by Augustan standards at a time when there was general discontent about their aptness or their sufficiency. Johnson was too great a man to be representative, too uncommon to stand for what was common to his age. And it follows that the impact of his personality upon his contemporaries and upon us derives from no adventitious circumstances but simply from an innate passionate force. This man who, as critic, insisted on the necessity for common sense to control the flights of imagination, was the same whose imagination so peopled his solitude that he implored his friends' company in the middle of the night. The man whose vivid emotional life is recorded in his private prayers, whose tender susceptibilities led him to maintain for years a household of waifs and strays and unfortunate eccentrics, is the same whose verses observe disciplines equalled in strictness only by Pope's. And this is not paradoxical. For it is the mind which knows the power of its own potentially disruptive propensities that needs and demands to be disciplined; and from another point of view, only an exceptionally powerful personality could successfully express itself in a verse-form, the heroic couplet, which a poet so great as Pope had so lately made peculiarly his own. Anyone would have thought that Pope had drawn out of that specialized instrument all the variety of which it was capable; Johnson reveals one string that none the less remained unplucked—gravity, sheer weight. There is personal experience pressed up close behind every abstraction; and a wealth of particular instances justifies every generalisation, though we know this only from the compactness and rigour of syntax, and the firmness of the metrical stress.

The circle of Johnson's friends, in particular that inner circle which at one period constituted itself 'the Club', included many —some eminent, some less so—of an individuality marked enough to make of them 'originals', strongly accented 'characters'. Even so, it could be maintained that the oddest figure of all in that milieu was OLIVER GOLDSMITH. But it would be more than odd, it would be unaccountable, if the Goldsmith whom Johnson admired and respected were the harmless zany whom Thackeray presents to us:

> What is the charm of his verse, of his style, and humour? His sweet regrets, his delicate compassion, his soft smile, his tremulous sympathy, the weakness which he owns? Your love for him is half pity. You come hot and tired from the day's battle, and this sweet minstrel sings to you. . . . He carries no weapon, save the harp on which he plays to you; and with which he delights

great and humble, young and old, the captains in the tents, or the soldiers round the fire, or the women and children in the villages, at whose porches he stops and sings his simple songs of love and beauty.

The flattery is flagrant. We, it is plain, are the captains of industry in the tents. It is we, the readers, who come from the battle and return to it. This fey child-like creature, the poet, is harmless; and his activity has nothing to do with the real business of life, which is the daily battle, our concern, fit work for authentic men. It comes as no surprise when, a little later in Thackeray's essay (it comes in his brilliantly misleading *English Humourists of the Eighteenth Century*), we find ourselves moving from a Goldsmith thus made in the image of his own Vicar of Wakefield, to Goldsmith the buffoon in the image of his own Tony Lumpkin, the inveigling hobbledehoy of *She Stoops to Conquer*. And yet there is some excuse for Thackeray. For the character of Goldsmith as we know it from anecdote and from his own writings (as essayist, playwright, novelist, and *vulgarisateur*, as well as poet) is extremely elusive and contradictory. Goldsmith must indeed have possessed something of the ineffectual charm of Dr. Primrose, something even of the impulsiveness and yokel shrewdness of Tony Lumpkin; yet his poems—*The Traveller* (1764) hardly less than *The Deserted Village*—forbid us to take either of these abstractions for the whole story. It was, one concludes, his adherence to Johnsonian standards which prevented him from exploiting in his essays—as Boswell was to do, and Charles Lamb—the lovingly elaborated idiosyncrasies of his own temperament; and it was the same standards by which he checked himself in his poetry from indulging a melancholy more authentic than that of the graveyard school or the sensibility-cult, a melancholy which in *The Deserted Village* for instance is not wholly accounted for by the passing of the civilisation which he laments, nor even by his nostalgia for his own lost boyhood in rural Ireland, but which inheres in the spectacle of the human condition as he observes it. It is unfair that just because Goldsmith suffered poverty as Thomas Gray didn't, lived from hand to mouth as a vagrant on the Continent, and toiled through Grub Street, we should be more affected by this 'white melancholy' in Goldsmith than as it shows itself in Gray, who similarly refused to exploit it. But it is not unfair to compare with Thackeray's wheedling of his public, the manliness of Letter 84 of *The Citizen of the World* (1762), where Goldsmith, having at no time made a comfortable living out of selling his wares on the open market, yet welcomes the passing of the system maintained for centuries by which the professional writer looked for a livelihood not to the public in general but to a patron. (This same epoch-making though gradual change in the economic status of the man of letters is, of course, the background to Johnson's dealings with Lord Chesterfield.)

Thackeray wants us to condescend to Goldsmith—'Your love for him is half pity.' Such condescension comes readily to all for whom the poet—so far from being exceptionally well-adjusted to reality—is by definition the man who cannot come to terms with it. And it is frequently invited by biographers for both Christopher Smart and WILLIAM COWPER. Goldsmith looked silly in company and couldn't manage his own money; Smart and Cowper ran mad. It is not easy to see what else Smart and Cowper have in common apart from their madness; and even in this they are not much alike, since Cowper's intermittent mental disease took the form of acute depression, whereas Smart's seems to have been characterised rather by unnatural elation and a conviction of groundless well-being. In both cases it is true that the mental state was coloured by religious 'enthusiasm' (in the eighteenth-century sense). And indeed it could hardly have been otherwise in an age when religious fervour, as distinct from doctrinal acuteness on the one hand and honest piety on the other, re-appeared in England after an absence of nearly a century. The careers of John Wesley and his collaborators sufficiently attest how rapid and powerful was this new impetus which rejuvenated the Established Church and the dissenting churches alike. There has been much discussion of how far Cowper's malady was caused by his contact with the Calvinist wing of this evangelical movement. The truth seems to be that he suffered from a congenital hypochondria which first led him to withdraw from public life, and it was the same morbid timidity which brought upon him his first fit of insanity. Cowper's malady may have been aggravated by the influence of John Newton, the Evangelical clergyman with whom he collaborated in the *Olney Hymns*. But it is obvious that Newton's God, whose power showed itself in electing to save some and damn others in ways that man finds arbitrary, would naturally appeal to Cowper as the most likely explanation of the special destiny of intermittent insanity to which he found himself condemned. Thus 'God moves in a mysterious way', has horrific implications. For what could be more mysterious to Cowper than the Act of God which brought about *The Loss of the Royal George,* lost with all hands when she capsized, not in battle nor in heavy weather at sea, but by the harbour wall? And Professor Kenneth Maclean has shown in a brilliant essay that many of Cowper's poems which seem tiresomely whimsical trivia about pet hares, caged finches, and cats who get shut in drawers, in fact show Cowper's God moving in just the same mysterious and horrifying way, His wrath seeking out even creatures leading unnaturally sheltered lives such as Cowper's own. Cowper's poetry thus raises in a particularly urgent way the question of how the biographer can or should help our appreciation of a poet's work. Without help from the biographer, Cowper's poems lose much of their point and poignancy. This is true not only of short lyrical pieces like *The Castaway*, but also of longer poems like *The Task* or *Friendship* or *Table Talk*. For these formally very conservative and late Augustan expressions of Horatian urbanity take on much extra significance when the reader knows they were written under the shadow of psychosis. As much can be said, indeed, even of *John Gilpin*, which at first sight witnesses only to genial high spirits. And when we know of Cowper's private infirmity, we admire him the more for having so resolutely turned his eyes away from his private world. We go to him for the fullest image in poetry of the public life of his times, and it is his patriotism, for instance, which reminds us that his was the England of the great explorers and navigators, Anson, Dampier, and Cook.

CHRISTOPHER SMART, because of the extraordinary vicissitudes of his disorganised life and the anecdotes about his eccentricities, has similarly attracted the biographer. But here the biographies and the anecdotes, far from illuminating the poetry, have only obscured it. The still common conviction (Romantic in origin) that the poet's vocation is necessarily at odds with all disciplines other than its own, and can flower only in rebellion and excess, has seemed to find conclusive illustration of this in the story of the brilliant Cambridge scholar who forfeited his fellowship through improvidence and dissipation, survived in the squalor and disorder of Grub Street, and went mad through a combination of religious mania and alcoholism. To crown the case it was convenient to suppose that the best poetry—in fact the only true poetry—came out of the madhouse. The indeed startling originality of *A Song to David*, the only poem by which Smart was generally known until quite lately, lent itself to this supposition. But the truth is that there is no evidence that this poem was written in insanity, and—what is more important—it is in any case distinguished by an astonishingly intricate and logical order, not by any sublimely disjointed afflatus. As recently as 1939 a much longer and unfinished poem which was indeed written in the asylum, *Jubilate Agno* ('Rejoice in the Lamb'), was published for the first time, and encouraged afresh the reading of Smart as a poet who was truly a poet only when out of his wits. But it has been proved by Mr. W. H. Bond that in the 1939 edition the poem was wrongly arranged, and that when restored to its original order much of its apparent waywardness disappears; though certainly the product of a disordered mind, this poem too turns out to have an intricate and rationally coherent plan— based on the antiphonal structure of Hebrew poetry, which Smart is known to have studied. Because many have tried to discredit the Age of Reason by maintaining, with Smart as prime example, that its poets were great only when their reason was gone, all the many poems which Smart wrote in complete lucidity, especially in his youth, have been neglected. Yet in all Smart's poems (and he was a very voluminous writer) he is never less than fresh and original, and he is frequently capable of sustained and astonishing beauty. This is as true of his work in conventional neo-classic forms like the ode and the couplet (octosyllabic or heroic), as in the novel forms he created for *A Song to David* and *Rejoice in the Lamb*. It is not impossible that when Smart is judged over the whole range of his various production—conventional in form as well as unconventional, light and even ribald as well as devotional, urbane or tender as well as sublime—he will be thought of as the greatest English poet between Pope and Wordsworth.

If it's important to maintain that Smart is not what a nine-teenth-century editor called him, 'Single-poem Smart' (the single memorable poem being *A Song to David*), it will be enough if we can establish 'Single-poem Langhorne' on the score of *The Country Justice*. So far as I know, this poem has not been reprinted for over a century, and though a modest claim might be made for other poems by JOHN LANGHORNE such as his *Owen of Carron*, it is *The Country Justice*, rather than its author or the whole body of his work, which demands to be rescued from oblivion. No one would claim that Langhorne's satirical couplets have any formal originality; it is necessary only to maintain that in *The Country Justice* he can, for a score of lines at a time, challenge and sustain comparison with his great predecessors in this genre, Pope and Johnson. In the following lines, on the absentee landlords of the countryfolk whose misery he laments, Langhorne puts between quotation marks a famous phrase from Gray's *Elegy*; but the pervasive influence is, of course, Pope (Pope here rather than Johnson, whose sarcasm is seldom so fast-moving and inventive):

> Foregone the social, hospitable Days,
> When wide Vales echoed with their Owner's Praise,
> Of all that *ancient Consequence* bereft,
> What has the *modern Man of Fashion left*?
>   Does He, perchance, to rural Scenes repair
> And 'waste his Sweetness' on the essenc'd Air?
> Ah! gently lave the feeble Frame He brings,
> Ye scouring Seas! and ye sulphureous Springs!
>   And thou, Brightelmstone, where no Cits annoy,
> (All borne to MARGATE, in the Margate-Hoy)
> Where, if the hasty Creditor advance,
> Lies the light Skiff, and ever-bailing France,
> Do Thou defend Him in the Dog-Day-Suns!
> Secure in Winter from the Rage of Duns!
>   While the grim Catchpole, the grim Porter swear,
> One that He is, and one, He is not there,
> The tortur'd Us'rer, as he murmurs by,
> Eyes the Venetian Blinds, and heaves a Sigh.

The third line, if one came across it quoted in all its plangency out of context, might well suggest, in sentiment and diction alike (the idiomatic use of 'consequence' for instance, its rippling syllables altering the metrical pace), the poetry of W. B. Yeats; the last source one would expect is an eighteenth-century satire in heroic couplets. And Gray's 'waste its sweetness on the desert air' is used as such quotations are used by Mr. Eliot, to create an extra irony by the contrast between its original context and the new one; for to the man of fashion the countryside is indeed a desert, where his accomplishments go for nothing, yet to the observer the rural air, being 'essenced' with flower-scents, has a sweetness in which it is the man's accomplishments that are barren like the desert. And in any case his breath stinks quite literally, a symptom of the diseases he has contracted through his excesses in the town. 'Ever-bailing' is another fine stroke, for 'bailing' has two senses. It is used in the sense of 'going bail' or 'out on bail'; but in such close conjunction with 'the light skiff', it recalls the other sense of the word as meaning what has to be done to keep afloat a leaky vessel, such as this man's health or his solvency. There is a witty surprise when the excessive word 'tortured' is applied not to the man of fashion himself but to the money-lender to whom he is in debt; and the wholly admirable vignette of the money-lender gives pleasure just because it is strictly speaking superfluous, a case of creative exuberance for good measure sketching rapidly in the margin. The vignette gets most of its vividness from the daring use of the verb, 'as he murmurs by'. I have argued else-where that it is typical of the best eighteenth-century verse to throw the weight of meaning and poetic energy on its verbs; this is a case in point. There is a similar effect, but more striking and elaborate, in the lines:

> More than all Asia's marmosets to view
> Grin, frisk, and water in the walks of Kew.

Here half the pleasure is in our feeling that there is no other context in which the three verbs, 'grin', 'frisk', and 'water', could come together and support each other as they do here. The effect resembles Smart's tremendous 'Determin'd, dared and done'; or Johnson's line on those favoured of Fortune:

> They mount, they shine, evaporate, and fall.

If one admits that none the less *The Country Justice* is more interesting for its subject than its style, this is not to say just that, in the lines quoted above for instance, Langhorne notes as a sign of the times the rise of the watering-place such as Brighton or Scarborough, seeing in it, as Cobbett and Jane Austen were to do afterwards, evidence of a morbid restlessness in metropolitan society; nor does one mean only to point out how *The Country Justice*, in its concern for rural vagrancy and destitution, is a link between *The Deserted Village* and the early poetry of Wordsworth (who admired this poem and Langhorne's work in general). Rather it is by realising how Langhorne in this poem had his finger on the pulse of his times, at the point where his society was feeling the strain of historical change, that one begins to appreciate his earnestness. For it is his earnestness, the urgency of his concern, which raises *The Country Justice* to a higher level than his other poems; and it is this which elevates him also above a satirist more naturally gifted with energy and command of the telling phrase, the profligate parson CHARLES CHURCHILL. For Churchill in none of his satires can maintain a consistent point of view as Langhorne does in *The Country Justice*; we weary of Churchill because we realise after a while that he is slashing indiscriminately, if trenchantly, at everything in sight. Langhorne's gaze is incomparably steadier. And it is natural to recall that Churchill was a figure of the metropolis, attacking corruption of political appointments, whereas Langhorne, another parson, born in Westmorland, spent most of his life in Yorkshire, Lincolnshire, and Somerset. It is one more case of the provincial figure being more in touch than the metropolitan.

The place for Wordsworth's *Old Cumberland Beggar* in this collection has already been defined; it is the natural culmination of a tradition in poetic subject matter to which *The Deserted Village* and *The Country Justice* also belong, as does *The Village*, of GEORGE CRABBE (1783). Wordsworth's eighteenth-century affinities are seldom noticed. For in the Preface to *Lyrical Ballads* Wordsworth himself seems to distinguish between the poetry he wrote himself and the poetry of the previous century as a whole. Yet Wordsworth is at least as much the last poet of the eighteenth century as the first of the nineteenth. This is not to minimize his profound originality, but it is important to realise where his originality lies. It does not lie in the first place in his 'technique', narrowly considered; for although, as he was aware himself, he made an experimental innovation of great importance in his use of a bare diction, in respect of imagery and versification he was at the time of *The Old Cumberland Beggar* quite conservative. Nor does his originality reside, where some have thought to find it, in his choice of a subject so humble as that of a rural beggar; for Langhorne and Shenstone, to name no more, had done the same. Wordsworth is original in his attitude to the subject, in making the light fall upon it from an unforeseen direction; in this instance, by treating the plight of the beggar, not from the beggar's standpoint, but from the point of view of the community which maintains him and so derives spiritual benefit from the beggar in its midst.

Wordsworth's Preface to *Lyrical Ballads*, hostile as it is to eighteenth-century poetry, is yet the best introduction to that poetry. For in trying to define its faults, Wordsworth also, unwittingly, indicates its virtues. When he declares, magnificently, 'The human mind is capable of being excited without the application of gross and violent stimulants', he voices what is a strong conviction of Johnson's also, of Goldsmith's, Langhorne's, Cowper's. In the subjects they choose and in their attitudes to those subjects, in their unwillingness to raise their voice above the tone of measured conversation, in their respect for common sense and a sense of proportion, they are all remarkable for sobriety. When Wordsworth spoke of 'the gaudiness and inane phraseology' of the writers of his time, he was maintaining in effect that this sobriety of outlook should be carried into, and reflected by, the very minutiae of poetic style. It was an insight of genius; and if Wordsworth's predecessors since Pope had not hit upon it, that is only to say, no doubt, that none of them had Wordsworth's genius. But it is more important to realise that in demanding sobriety of style and diction Wordsworth was only carrying one stage further a rejection of 'gross and violent stimulants' which is already implicit in the subjects and the attitudes of Langhorne and Cowper and the others. In this too—paradoxical as it may seem—Wordsworth is rather the last poet of the eighteenth century than the first of the nineteenth.

DONALD DAVIE

Trinity College,
  Dublin.

POEMS

WILLIAM SHENSTONE

The School-Mistress

In Imitation of SPENSER

Auditae voces, vagitus & ingens,
Infantumque animae flentes in Limine primo.

VIRG.

ADVERTISEMENT.

What particulars in Spenser were imagin'd most proper for the Author's imitation on *this occasion*, are his *language*, his *simplicity*, his manner of *description*, and a peculiar *tenderness* of *sentiment* remarkable throughout his works.

I

Ah me! full sorely is my heart forlorn,
To think how modest worth neglected lies;
While partial Fame doth with her blasts adorn
Such deeds alone as pride and pomp disguise;
Deeds of ill sort, and mischievous emprize!
Lend me thy clarion, goddess! let me try
To sound the praise of merit, ere it dies;
Such as I oft have chaunced to espy,
Lost in the dreary shades of dull obscurity.

In ev'ry village mark'd with little spire,
Embow'r'd in trees, and hardly known to Fame,
There dwells, in lowly shed, and mean attire,
A matron old, whom we school-mistress name;
Who boasts unruly brats with birch to tame.
They grieven sore, in piteous durance pent,
Aw'd by the pow'r of this relentless dame;
And oft-times, on vagaries idly bent,
For unkempt hair, or task unconn'd, are sorely shent.

3

And all in sight doth rise a birchen tree,
Which Learning near her little dome did stowe;
Whilom a twig of small regard to see,
Tho' now so wide its waving branches flow;
And work the simple vassals mickle woe;
For not a wind might curl the leaves that blew,
But their limbs shudder'd, and their pulse beat low;
And, as they look'd, they found their horror grew,
And shap'd it into rods, and tingled at the view.

4

So have I seen (who has not may conceive,)
A lifeless phantom near a garden plac'd:
So doth it wanton birds of peace bereave,
Of sport, of song, of pleasure, of repast;
They start, they stare, they wheel, they look aghast:
Sad servitude! such comfortless annoy
May no bold Briton's riper age e'er taste!
Ne Superstition clog his dance of joy,
Ne vision empty, vain, his native bliss destroy.

5

Near to this dome is found a patch so green,
On which the tribe their gambols do display;
And at the door impris'ning board is seen,
Lest weakly wights of smaller size should stray;
Eager, perdie, to bask in sunny day!
The noises intermix'd, which thence resound,
Do Learning's little tenement betray:
Where sits the dame, disguis'd in look profound,
And eyes her fairy throng, and turns her wheel around.

6

Her cap, far whiter than the driven snow,
Emblem right meet of decency does yield:
Her apron dy'd in grain, as blue, I trowe,
As is the hare-bell that adorns the field:
And in her hand, for scepter, she does wield
Tway birchen sprays; with anxious Fear entwin'd,
With dark Distrust, and sad Repentance fill'd;
And stedfast hate, and sharp Affliction join'd,
And Fury uncontroul'd, and Chastisement unkind.

7

Few but have ken'd, in semblance meet pourtray'd,
The childish faces of old EOL's train;
LIBS, NOTUS, AUSTER: these in frowns array'd,
How then would fare or earth, or sky, or main,
Were the stern god to give his slaves the rein?
And were not she rebellious breasts to quell,
And were not she her statutes to maintain,
The cott no more, I ween, were deem'd the cell,
Where comely peace of mind, and decent order dwell.

8

A russet stole was o'er her shoulders thrown;
A russet kirtle fenc'd the nipping air;
'Twas simple russet, but it was her own;
'Twas her own country bred the flock so fair;
'Twas her own labour did the fleece prepare;
And, sooth to say, her pupils, rang'd around,
Thro' pious awe, did term it passing rare;
For they in gaping wonderment abound,
And think, no doubt, she been the greatest wight on ground.

9

Albeit ne flatt'ry did corrupt her truth,
Ne pompous title did debauch her ear;
Goody, good-woman, gossip, n'aunt, forsooth,
Or dame, the sole additions she did hear;
Yet these she challeng'd, these she held right dear:
Ne would esteem him act as mought behove,
Who should not honour'd eld with these revere:
For never title yet so mean could prove,
But there was eke a Mind which did that title love.

10

One ancient hen she took delight to feed,
The plodding pattern of the busy dame;
Which, ever and anon, impell'd by need,
Into her school, begirt with chickens, came;
Such favour did her past deportment claim:
And, if Neglect had lavish'd on the ground
Fragment of bread, she would collect the same;
For well she knew, and quaintly could expound,
What sin it were to waste the smallest crumb she found.

11

Herbs too she knew, and well of each could speak,
That in her garden sip'd the silv'ry dew;
Where no vain flow'r disclos'd a gawdy streak;
But herbs for use, and physick, not a few,
Of grey renown, within those borders grew:
The tufted Basil, pun-provoking Thyme,
Fresh Baum, and Mary-gold of chearful hue;
The lowly Gill, that never dares to climb;
And more I fain would sing, disdaining here to rhyme.

12

Yet Euphrasy may not be left unsung,
That gives dim eyes to wander leagues around;
And pungent Radish, biting infant's tongue;
And Plantain ribb'd, that heals the reaper's wound;
And Marj'ram sweet, in shepherd's posie found;
And Lavender, whose spikes of azure bloom
Shall be, ere-while, in arid bundles bound,
To lurk amidst the labours of her loom,
And crown her kerchiefs clean, with mickle rare perfume

13

And here trim Rosmarine, that whilom crown'd
The daintiest garden of the proudest peer;
Ere, driven from its envy'd site, it found
A sacred shelter for its branches here;
Where edg'd with gold its glitt'ring skirts appear.
Oh wassel days; O customs meet and well!
Ere this was banish'd from its lofty sphere:
Simplicity then sought this humble cell,
Nor ever would She more with thane and lordling dwell.

14

Here oft the dame, on Sabbath's decent eve,
Hymned such psalms as STERNHOLD forth did mete,
If winter 'twere, she to her hearth did cleave;
But in her garden found a summer seat:
Sweet melody! to hear her then repeat
How ISRAEL's sons, beneath a foreign king,
While taunting foe-men did a song intreat,
All for the nonce, untuning ev'ry string,
Uphung their useless lyres—small heart had they to sing.

15

For she was just, and friend to virtuous lore,
And pass'd much time in truly virtuous deed;
And in those Elfins' ears, would oft deplore
The times, when Truth by popish rage did bleed;
And tortious death was true Devotion's meed;
And simple Faith in iron chains did mourn,
That nould on wooden image place her creed;
And lawny saints in smould'ring flames did burn:
Ah! dearest Lord, forefend, thilk days should e'er return.

16

In elbow chair, like that of Scottish stem
By the sharp tooth of cank'ring eld defac'd,
In which, when he receives his diadem,
Our sovereign prince and liefest liege is plac'd,
The matron sate; and some with rank she grac'd,
(The source of children's and of courtier's pride!)
Redress'd affronts, for vile affronts there pass'd;
And warn'd them not the fretful to deride,
But love each other dear, whatever them betide.

Right well she knew each temper to descry;
To thwart the proud, and the submiss to raise;
Some with vile copper prize exalt on high,
And some entice with pittance small of praise;
And other some with baleful sprig she 'frays;
Ev'n absent, she the reins of pow'r doth hold,
While with quaint arts the giddy crowd she sways;
Forewarn'd, if little bird their pranks behold,
'Twill whisper in her ear, and all the scene unfold.

18

Lo now with state she utters the command!
Eftsoons the urchins to their tasks repair:
Their books of stature small they take in hand,
Which with pellucid horn secured are,
To save from finger wet the letters fair:
The work so gay, that on their back is seen,
St. GEORGE's high atchievements does declare;
On which thilk wight that has y-gazing been,
Kens the forth-coming rod, unpleasing sight, I ween

Ah luckless he, and born beneath the beam
Of evil star! it irks me whilst I write!
As erst the bard by MULLA's silver stream,
Oft, as he told of deadly dolorous plight,
Sigh'd as he sung, and did in tears indite.
For brandishing the rod, she doth begin
To loose the brogues, the stripling's late delight!
And down they drop; appears his dainty skin,
Fair as the furry coat of whiten Ermilin.

O ruthful scene! when from a nook obscure,
His little sister doth his peril see:
All playful as she sate, she grows demure;
She finds full soon her wonted spirits flee:
She meditates a pray'r to set him free:
Nor gentle pardon could this dame deny,
(If gentle pardon could with dames agree)
To her sad grief that swells in either eye,
And wrings her so that all for pity she could dye.

Nor longer can she now her shrieks command;
And hardly she forbears, thro' aweful fear,
To rushen forth, and, with presumptuous hand,
To stay harsh justice in its mid career.
On thee she calls, on thee her parent dear!
(Ah! too remote to ward the shameful blow!)
She sees no kind domestic visage near,
And soon a flood of tears begins to flow;
And gives a loose at last to unavailing woe.

But ah! what pen his piteous plight may trace?
Or what device his loud laments explain?
The form uncouth of his disguisèd face?
The pallid hue that dyes his looks amain?
The plenteous show'r that does his cheek distain?
When he, in abject wise, implores the dame,
Ne hopeth aught of sweet reprieve to gain;
Or when from high she levels well her aim,
And, thro' the thatch, his cries each falling stroke proclaim.

The other tribe, aghast, with sore dismay,
Attend, and conn their tasks with mickle care:
By turns, astony'd, ev'ry twig survey,
And, from their fellow's hateful wounds, beware;
Knowing, I wist, how each the same may share;
'Till Fear has taught them a performance meet,
And to the well-known chest the dame repair;
Whence oft with sugar'd cates she doth 'em greet,
And ginger-bread y-rare; now, certes, doubly sweet!

See to their seats they hye with merry glee,
And in beseemly order sitten there;
All but the wight of bum y-gallèd, he
Abhorreth bench and stool, and fourm, and chair;
(This hand in mouth y-fix'd, that rends his hair;)
And eke with snubs profound, and heaving breast,
Convulsions intermitting! does declare
His grievous wrong; his dame's unjust behest;
And scorns her offer'd love, and shuns to be caress'd.

His face besprent with liquid crystal shines,
His blooming face that seems a purple flow'r,
Which low to earth its drooping head declines,
All smear'd and sully'd by a vernal show'r.
O the hard bosoms of despotic pow'r!
All, all, but she, the author of his shame,
All, all, but she, regret this mournful hour:
Yet hence the youth, and hence the flow'r, shall claim,
If so I deem aright, transcending worth and fame.

Behind some door, in melancholy thought,
Mindless of food, he, dreary caitiff! pines;
Ne for his fellow's joyaunce careth aught,
But to the wind all merriment resigns;
And deems it shame, if he to peace inclines;
And many a sullen look ascance is sent,
Which for his dame's annoyance he designs;
And still the more to pleasure him she's bent,
The more doth he, perverse, her haviour past resent.

27

Ah me! how much I fear lest pride it be!
But if that pride it be, which thus inspires,
Beware, ye dames, with nice discernment see,
Ye quench not too the sparks of nobler fires:
Ah! better far than all the Muses' lyres,
All coward arts, is valour's gen'rous heat;
The firm fixt breast which Fit and Right requires,
Like VERNON's patriot soul; more justly great
Than craft that pimps for ill, or flow'ry false deceit.

28

Yet nurs'd with skill, what dazling fruits appear!
Ev'n now sagacious Foresight points to show
A little bench of heedless bishops here,
And there a chancellour in embryo,
Or bard sublime, if bard may e'er be so,
As MILTON, SHAKESPEAR, names that ne'er shall dye
Tho now he crawl along the ground so low,
Nor weeting how the Muse should soar on high,
Wisheth, poor starv'ling elf! his paper-kite may fly.

And this perhaps, who, cens'ring the design,
Low lays the house which that of cards doth build,
Shall DENNIS be! if rigid fates incline,
And many an Epic to his rage shall yield;
And many a poet quit th' Aonian field;
And, sour'd by age, profound he shall appear,
As he who now with 'sdainful fury thrill'd
Surveys mine work; and levels many a sneer,
And furls his wrinkly front, and cries, 'What stuff is here?'

30

But now DAN PHOEBUS gains the middle skie,
And Liberty unbars their prison-door;
And like a rushing torrent out they fly,
And now the grassy cirque han cover'd o'er
With boist'rous revel-rout and wild uproar;
A thousand ways in wanton rings they run,
Heav'n shield their short liv'd pastimes, I implore!
For well may Freedom, erst so dearly won,
Appear to British elf more gladsome than the sun.

31

Enjoy, poor imps! enjoy your sportive trade;
And chase gay flies, and cull the fairest flow'rs
For when my bones in grass-green sods are laid;
For never may ye taste more careless hours
In knightly castles, or in ladies bow'rs.
O vain to seek delight in earthly thing!
But most in courts where proud Ambition tow'rs;
Deluded wight! who weens fair peace can spring
Beneath the pompous dome of kesar or of king.

See in each sprite some various bent appear!
These rudely carol most incondite lay;
Those saunt'ring on the green, with jocund leer
Salute the stranger passing on his way;
Some builden fragile tenements of clay;
Some to the standing lake their courses bend,
With pebbles smooth at duck and drake to play;
Thilk to the huxter's sav'ry cottage tend,
In pastry kings and queens th' allotted mite to spend.

33

Here, as each season yields a different store,
Each season's stores in order rangèd been;
Apples with cabbage-net y-cover'd o'er,
Galling full sore th' unmoney'd wight, are seen;
And goose-b'rie clad in liv'ry red or green;
And here of lovely dye, the Cath'rine pear,
Fine pear! as lovely for thy juice, I ween:
O may no wight e'er pennyless come there,
Lest smit with ardent love he pine with hopeless care!

34

See! cherries here, ere cherries yet abound,
With thread so white in tempting posies ty'd,
Scatt'ring like blooming maid their glances round,
With pamper'd look draw little eyes aside;
And must be bought, tho' penury betide.
The plum all azure and the nut all brown,
And here each season, do those cakes abide,
Whose honour'd names th'inventive city own,
Rend'ring thro' Britain's isle SALOPIA's praises known.

Admir'd SALOPIA! that with venial pride
Eyes her bright form in SEVERN's ambient wave,
Fam'd for her loyal cares in perils try'd,
Her daughters lovely, and her striplings brave;
Ah! midst the rest, may flowers adorn his grave,
Whose art did first these dulcet cates display!
A motive fair to Learning's imps he gave,
Who chearless o'er her darkling region stray;
'Till reason's morn arise, and light them on their way.

SAMUEL JOHNSON

The Vanity of Human Wishes

In imitation of the Tenth Satire of Juvenal

Let observation, with extensive view,
Survey mankind, from China to Peru;
Remark each anxious toil, each eager strife,
And watch the busy scenes of crowded life;
Then say how hope and fear, desire and hate,   5
O'erspread with snares the clouded maze of fate,
Where wav'ring man, betray'd by vent'rous pride,
To tread the dreary paths without a guide,
As treach'rous phantoms in the mist delude,
Shuns fancied ills, or chases airy good.   10
How rarely reason guides the stubborn choice,
Rules the bold hand, or prompts the suppliant voice;
How nations sink, by darling schemes oppress'd,
When vengeance listens to the fool's request.
Fate wings with ev'ry wish th' afflictive dart,   15
Each gift of nature, and each grace of art;
With fatal heat impetuous courage glows,
With fatal sweetness elocution flows;
Impeachment stops the speaker's pow'rful breath,
And restless fire precipitates on death.   20
But scarce observ'd, the knowing and the bold
Fall in the gen'ral massacre of gold;
Wide-wasting pest! that rages unconfin'd,
And crowds with crimes the records of mankind;

For gold his sword the hireling ruffian draws,   25
For gold the hireling judge distorts the laws;
Wealth heap'd on wealth, nor truth nor safety buys,
The dangers gather as the treasures rise.
   Let hist'ry tell where rival kings command,
And dubious title shakes the madded land,   30
When statutes glean the refuse of the sword,
How much more safe the vassal than the lord;
Low skulks the hind beneath the rage of pow'r,
And leaves the wealthy traitor in the Tow'r,
Untouch'd his cottage, and his slumbers sound,   35
Tho' confiscation's vultures hover round.
   The needy traveller, serene and gay,
Walks the wild heath, and sings his toil away.
Does envy seize thee? crush th' upbraiding joy,
Increase his riches, and his peace destroy;   40
New fears in dire vicissitude invade,
The rustling brake alarms and quiv'ring shade;
Nor light nor darkness bring his pain relief,
One shews the plunder, and one hides the thief.
   Yet still one gen'ral cry the skies assails,   45
And gain and grandeur load the tainted gales;
Few know the toiling statesman's fear or care,
Th' insidious rival and the gaping heir.
   Once more, Democritus, arise on earth,
With cheerful wisdom and instructive mirth,   50
See motley life in modern trappings dress'd,
And feed with varied fools th' eternal jest:
Thou who couldst laugh where want enchain'd caprice,
Toil crush'd conceit, and man was of a piece;
Where wealth unlov'd without a mourner dy'd;   55
And scarce a sycophant was fed by pride;
Where ne'er was known the form of mock debate,
Or seen a new-made mayor's unwieldy state;
Where change of fav'rites made no change of laws,

And senates heard before they judg'd a cause;   60
How wouldst thou shake at Britain's modish tribe,
Dart the quick taunt, and edge the piercing gibe?
Attentive truth and nature to descry,
And pierce each scene with philosophic eye.
To thee were solemn toys or empty show,   65
The robes of pleasure and the veils of woe:
All aid the force, and all thy mirth maintain,
Whose joys are causeless, or whose griefs are vain.
    Such was the scorn that fill'd the sage's mind,
Renew'd at ev'ry glance on human kind;   70
How just that scorn ere yet thy voice declare,
Search every state, and canvass ev'ry pray'r.
    Unnumber'd suppliants crowd Preferment's gate,
Athirst for wealth, and burning to be great;
Delusive Fortune hears th' incessant call,   75
They mount, they shine, evaporate, and fall.
On ev'ry stage the foes of peace attend,
Hate dogs their flight, and insult mocks their end.
Love ends with hope, the sinking statesman's door
Pours in the morning worshipper no more;   80
For growing names the weekly scribbler lies,
To growing wealth the dedicator flies;
From ev'ry room descends the painted face,
That hung the bright Palladium of the place,
And smok'd in kitchens, or in auctions sold,   85
To better features yields the frame of gold;
For now no more we trace in ev'ry line
Heroic worth, benevolence divine:
The form distorted justifies the fall,
And detestation rids th' indignant wall.   90
    But will not Britain hear the last appeal,
Sign her foes' doom, or guard her fav'rites' zeal?
Thro' Freedom's sons no more remonstrance rings,
Degrading nobles and controlling kings;

Our supple tribes repress their patriot throats,   95
And ask no questions but the price of votes;
With weekly libels and septennial ale,
Their wish is full to riot and to rail.
  In full-blown dignity, see Wolsey stand,
Law in his voice, and fortune in his hand: 100
To him the church, the realm, their pow'rs consign,
Thro' him the rays of regal bounty shine,
Still to new heights his restless wishes tow'r,
Claim leads to claim, and pow'r advances pow'r;
Till conquest unresisted ceas'd to please,   105
And rights submitted, left him none to seize.
At length his sovereign frowns—the train of state
Mark the keen glance, and watch the sign to hate.
Where'er he turns he meets a stranger's eye,
His suppliants scorn him, and his followers fly;   110
At once is lost the pride of awful state,
The golden canopy, the glitt'ring plate,
The regal palace, the luxurious board,
The liv'ried army, and the menial lord.
With age, with cares, with maladies oppress'd,   115
He seeks the refuge of monastic rest.
Grief aids disease, remember'd folly stings,
And his last sighs reproach the faith of kings.
  Speak thou, whose thoughts at humble peace repine,
Shall Wolsey's wealth, with Wolsey's end, be thine?   120
Or liv'st thou now, with safer pride content,
The wisest justice on the banks of Trent?
For why did Wolsey near the steeps of fate,
On weak foundations raise th' enormous weight?
Why but to sink beneath misfortune's blow,   125
With louder ruin to the gulphs below?
  What gave great Villiers to th' assassin's knife,
And fix'd disease on Harley's closing life?
What murder'd Wentworth, and what exil'd Hyde,

By kings protected, and to kings ally'd?   130
What but their wish indulg'd in courts to shine,
And pow'r too great to keep, or to resign?
    When first the college rolls receive his name,
The young enthusiast quits his ease for fame;
Through all his veins the fever of renown   135
Burns from the strong contagion of the gown;
O'er Bodley's dome his future labours spread,
And Bacon's mansion trembles o'er his head.
Are these thy views? proceed, illustrious youth,
And Virtue guard thee to the throne of Truth!   140
Yet should thy soul indulge the gen'rous heat,
Till captive Science yields her last retreat;
Should Reason guide thee with her brightest ray,
And pour on misty Doubt resistless day;
Should no false Kindness lure to loose delight,   145
Nor Praise relax, nor Difficulty fright;
Should tempting Novelty thy cell refrain,
And Sloth effuse her opiate fumes in vain;
Should Beauty blunt on fops her fatal dart,
Nor claim the triumph of a letter'd heart;   150
Should no Disease thy torpid veins invade,
Nor Melancholy's phantoms haunt thy shade;
Yet hope not life from grief or danger free,
Nor think the doom of man revers'd for thee:
Deign on the passing world to turn thine eyes,   155
And pause awhile from letters, to be wise;
There mark what ills the scholar's life assail,
Toil, envy, want, the patron, and the jail.
See nations slowly wise, and meanly just,
To buried merit raise the tardy bust.   160
If dreams yet flatter, once again attend,
Hear Lydiat's life, and Galileo's end.
    Nor deem, when Learning her last prize bestows,
The glitt'ring eminence exempt from woes;

See when the vulgar 'scape, despis'd or aw'd,   165
Rebellion's vengeful talons seize on Laud.
From meaner minds, tho' smaller fines content,
The plunder'd palace or sequester'd rent;
Mark'd out by dang'rous parts he meets the shock,
And fatal Learning leads him to the block: 170
Around his tomb let Art and Genius weep,
But hear his death, ye blockheads, hear and sleep.
   The festal blazes, the triumphal show,
The ravish'd standard, and the captive foe,
The senate's thanks, the gazette's pompous tale,   175
With force resistless o'er the brave prevail.
Such bribes the rapid Greek o'er Asia whirl'd,
For such the steady Romans shook the world;
For such in distant lands the Britons shine,
And stain with blood the Danube or the Rhine;   180
This pow'r has praise, that virtue scarce can warm,
Till fame supplies the universal charm.
Yet Reason frowns on War's unequal game,
Where wasted nations raise a single name,
And mortgag'd states their grandsires' wreaths regret,   185
From age to age in everlasting debt;
Wreaths which at last the dear-bought right convey
To rust on medals, or on stones decay.
   On what foundation stands the warrior's pride,
How just his hopes, let Swedish Charles decide;   190
A frame of adamant, a soul of fire,
No dangers fright him, and no labours tire;
O'er love, o'er fear, extends his wide domain,
Unconquer'd lord of pleasure and of pain;
No joys to him pacific sceptres yield,   195
War sounds the trump, he rushes to the field;
Behold surrounding kings their pow'rs combine,
And one capitulate, and one resign;
Peace courts his hand, but spreads her charms in vain;

'Think nothing gain'd,' he cries, 'till nought remain,   200
On Moscow's walls till Gothic standards fly,
And all be mine beneath the polar sky.'
The march begins in military state,
And nations on his eye suspended wait;
Stern Famine guards the solitary coast,   205
And Winter barricades the realms of Frost;
He comes, nor want nor cold his course delay;—
Hide, blushing Glory, hide Pultowa's day:
The vanquish'd hero leaves his broken bands,
And shews his miseries in distant lands;   210
Condemn'd a needy supplicant to wait,
While ladies interpose, and slaves debate.
But did not Chance at length her error mend?
Did no subverted empire mark his end?
Did rival monarchs give the fatal wound?   215
Or hostile millions press him to the ground?
His fall was destin'd to a barren strand,
A petty fortress, and a dubious hand;
He left the name, at which the world grew pale,
To point a moral, or adorn a tale.   220
    All times their scenes of pompous woes afford,
From Persia's tyrant, to Bavaria's lord.
In gay hostility, and barb'rous pride,
With half mankind embattled at his side,
Great Xerxes comes to seize the certain prey,   225
And starves exhausted regions in his way;
Attendant Flatt'ry counts his myriads o'er,
Till counted myriads soothe his pride no more;
Fresh praise is try'd till madness fires his mind,
The waves he lashes, and enchains the wind;   230
New pow'rs are claim'd, new pow'rs are still bestow'd,
Till rude resistance lops the spreading god;
The daring Greeks deride the martial show,
And heap their valleys with the gaudy foe;

Th' insulted sea with humbler thoughts he gains,   235
A single skiff to speed his flight remains;
Th' incumber'd oar scarce leaves the dreaded coast
Through purple billows and a floating host.
    The bold Bavarian, in a luckless hour,
Tries the dread summits of Caesarian pow'r,   240
With unexpected legions bursts away,
And sees defenceless realms receive his sway;
Short sway! fair Austria spreads her mournful charms,
The queen, the beauty, sets the world in arms;
From hill to hill the beacons' rousing blaze   245
Spreads wide the hope of plunder and of praise;
The fierce Croatian, and the wild Hussar,
And all the sons of ravage crowd the war;
The baffled prince in honour's flatt'ring bloom
Of hasty greatness finds the fatal doom,   250
His foes derision, and his subjects blame.
And steals to death from anguish and from shame.
    Enlarge my life with multitude of days,
In health, in sickness, thus the suppliant prays;
Hides from himself his state, and shuns to know,   255
That life protracted, is protracted woe.
Time hovers o'er, impatient to destroy,
And shuts up all the passages of joy:
In vain their gifts the bounteous seasons pour,
The fruit autumnal, and the vernal flow'r,   260
With listless eyes the dotard views the store,
He views, and wonders that they please no more;
Now pall the tasteless meats, and joyless wines,
And Luxury with sighs her slave resigns.
Approach, ye minstrels, try the soothing strain,   265
And yield the tuneful lenitives of pain:
No sounds, alas, would touch th' impervious ear
Though dancing mountains witness'd Orpheus near;
Nor lute nor lyre his feeble pow'rs attend,

Nor sweeter musick of a virtuous friend,   270
But everlasting dictates crowd his tongue,
Perversely grave or positively wrong.
The still returning tale, and ling'ring jest,
Perplex the fawning niece and pamper'd guest,
While growing hopes scarce awe the gath'ring sneer,   275
And scarce a legacy can bribe to hear;
The watchful guests still hint the last offence,
The daughter's petulance, the son's expence,
Improve his heady rage with treach'rous skill,
And mould his passions till they make his will.   280
    Unnumber'd maladies his joints invade,
Lay siege to life, and press the dire blockade;
But unextinguish'd Av'rice still remains,
And dreaded losses aggravate his pains;
He turns, with anxious heart and crippled hands,   285
His bonds of debt, and mortgages of lands;
Or views his coffers with suspicious eyes,
Unlocks his gold, and counts it till he dies.
    But grant, the virtues of a temp'rate prime
Bless with an age exempt from scorn or crime;   290
An age that melts in unperceiv'd decay,
And glides in modest innocence away;
Whose peaceful day Benevolence endears,
Whose night congratulating Conscience cheers;
The gen'ral fav'rite as the gen'ral friend: 295
Such age there is, and who could wish its end?
    Yet ev'n on this her load Misfortune flings,
To press the weary minutes' flagging wings:
New sorrow rises as the day returns,
A sister sickens, or a daughter mourns.   300
Now kindred Merit fills the sable bier,
Now lacerated Friendship claims a tear.
Year chases year, decay pursues decay,
Still drops some joy from with'ring life away;

New forms arise, and diff'rent views engage,   305
Superfluous lags the vet'ran on the stage,
Till pitying Nature signs the last release,
And bids afflicted worth retire to peace.
    But few there are whom hours like these await,
Who set unclouded in the gulphs of Fate.   310
From Lydia's monarch should the search descend,
By Solon caution'd to regard his end,
In life's last scene what prodigies surprise,
Fears of the brave, and follies of the wise?
From Marlb'rough's eyes the streams of dotage flow,   315
And Swift expires a driv'ler and a show.
    The teeming mother, anxious for her race,
Begs for each birth the fortune of a face:
Yet Vane could tell what ills from beauty spring;
And Sedley curs'd the form that pleas'd a king.   320
Ye nymphs of rosy lips and radiant eyes,
Whom Pleasure keeps too busy to be wise,
Whom Joys with soft varieties invite,
By day the frolick, and the dance by night,
Who frown with vanity, who smile with art,   325
And ask the latest fashion of the heart,
What care, what rules your heedless charms shall save,
Each nymph your rival, and each youth your slave?
Against your fame with fondness hate combines,
The rival batters, and the lover mines.   330
With distant voice neglected Virtue calls,
Less heard and less, the faint remonstrance falls;
Tir'd with contempt, she quits the slipp'ry reign,
And Pride and Prudence take her seat in vain.
In crowd at once, where none the pass defend,   335
The harmless Freedom, and the private Friend.
The guardians yield, by force superior ply'd;
To int'rest, Prudence; and to Flatt'ry, Pride.
Now Beauty falls betray'd, despis'd, distress'd,

And hissing Infamy proclaims the rest.   340
    Where then shall Hope and Fear their objects find?
Must dull Suspense corrupt the stagnant mind?
Must helpless man, in ignorance sedate,
Roll darkling down the torrent of his fate?
Must no dislike alarm, no wishes rise   345
No cries attempt the mercies of the skies?
Inquirer, cease, petitions yet remain,
Which heav'n may hear, nor deem religion vain.
Still raise for good the supplicating voice,
But leave to heav'n the measure and the choice.   350
Safe in his pow'r, whose eyes discern afar
The secret ambush of a specious pray'r,
Implore his aid, in his decisions rest,
Secure whate'er he gives, he gives the best.
Yet when the sense of sacred presence fires,   355
And strong devotion to the skies aspires,
Pour forth thy fervours for a healthful mind,
Obedient passions, and a will resign'd;
For love, which scarce collective man can fill;
For patience, sov'reign o'er transmuted ill;   360
For faith, that, panting for a happier seat,
Counts death kind Nature's signal of retreat:
These goods for man the laws of heav'n ordain,
These goods he grants, who grants the pow'r to gain;
With these celestial Wisdom calms the mind,   365
And makes the happiness she does not find.

THOMAS GRAY

Elegy

Written in a Country Churchyard

1

The curfew tolls the knell of parting day,
The lowing herd wind slowly o'er the lea,
The ploughman homeward plods his weary way,
And leaves the world to darkness and to me.

2

Now fades the glimmering landscape on the sight,
And all the air a solemn stillness holds,
Save where the beetle wheels his droning flight,
And drowsy tinklings lull the distant folds;

3

Save that from yonder ivy-mantled tower,
The moping owl does to the moon complain
Of such, as wandering near her secret bower,
Molest her ancient solitary reign.

4

Beneath those rugged elms, that yew-tree's shade,
Where heaves the turf in many a mould'ring heap,
Each in his narrow cell for ever laid,
The rude forefathers of the hamlet sleep.

5

The breezy call of incense-breathing Morn,
The swallow twitt'ring from the straw-built shed,
The cock's shrill clarion, or the echoing horn,
No more shall rouse them from their lowly bed.

6

For them no more the blazing hearth shall burn,
Or busy housewife ply her evening care:
No children run to lisp their sire's return,
Or climb his knees the envied kiss to share.

7

Oft did the harvest to their sickle yield,
Their furrow oft the stubborn glebe has broke;
How jocund did they drive their team afield!
How bowed the woods beneath their sturdy stroke!

8

Let not Ambition mock their useful toil,
Their homely joys, and destiny obscure;
Nor Grandeur hear with a disdainful smile,
The short and simple annals of the poor.

9

The boast of heraldry, the pomp of power,
And all that beauty, all that wealth e'er gave,
Await alike th' inevitable hour:
The paths of glory lead but to the grave.

10

Nor you, ye proud, impute to these the fault,
If Memory o'er their tomb no trophies raise,
Where thro' the long-drawn aisle and fretted vault
The pealing anthem swells the note of praise.

11

Can storied urn or animated bust
Back to its mansion call the fleeting breath?
Can Honour's voice provoke the silent dust,
Or Flatt'ry soothe the dull cold ear of death?

12

Perhaps in this neglected spot is laid
Some heart once pregnant with celestial fire;
Hands, that the rod of empire might have sway'd,
Or waked to extasy the living lyre.

13

But Knowledge to their eyes her ample page
Rich with the spoils of time did ne'er unroll;
Chill Penury repress'd their noble rage,
And froze the genial current of the soul.

14

Full many a gem of purest ray serene,
The dark unfathom'd caves of ocean bear:
Full many a flower is born to blush unseen,
And waste its sweetness on the desert air.

15

Some village-Hampden, that with dauntless breast
The little tyrant of his fields withstood;
Some mute inglorious Milton here may rest,
Some Cromwell, guiltless of his country's blood.

16

Th' applause of listening senates to command,
The threats of pain and ruin to despise,
To scatter plenty o'er a smiling land,
And read their history in a nation's eyes,

Their lot forbad: nor circumscribed alone
Their growing virtues, but their crimes confined;
Forbad to wade through slaughter to a throne,
And shut the gates of mercy on mankind;

The struggling pangs of conscious truth to hide,
To quench the blushes of ingenuous shame,
Or heap the shrine of Luxury and Pride
With incense kindled at the Muse's flame.

Far from the madding crowd's ignoble strife,
Their sober wishes never learn'd to stray;
Along the cool sequester'd vale of life
They kept the noiseless tenour of their way.

Yet ev'n these bones from insult to protect
Some frail memorial still erected nigh,
With uncouth rhymes and shapeless sculpture decked,
Implores the passing tribute of a sigh.

Their name, their years, spelt by th' unletter'd Muse,
The place of fame and elegy supply:
And many a holy text around she strews,
That teach the rustic moralist to die.

For who, to dumb Forgetfulness a prey,
This pleasing anxious being e'er resign'd,
Left the warm precincts of the cheerful day,
Nor cast one longing lingering look behind?

On some fond breast the parting soul relies,
Some pious drops the closing eye requires;
E'en from the tomb the voice of Nature cries,
E'en in our Ashes live their wonted fires.

For thee, who, mindful of th' unhonour'd dead,
Dost in these lines their artless tale relate;
If chance, by lonely contemplation led,
Some kindred spirit shall inquire thy fate,—

Haply some hoary-headed Swain may say,
' Oft have we seen him at the peep of dawn
Brushing with hasty steps the dews away
To meet the sun upon the upland lawn.

'There at the foot of yonder nodding beech
That wreathes its old fantastic roots so high
His listless length at noontide would he stretch,
And pore upon the brook that babbles by.

'Hard by yon wood, now smiling as in scorn
Muttering his wayward fancies he would rove;
Now drooping, woeful wan, like one forlorn,
Or crazed with care, or cross'd in hopeless love.

'One morn I missed him on the custom'd hill,
Along the heath and near his favourite tree;
Another came; nor yet beside the rill,
Nor up the lawn, nor at the wood was he;

'The next, with dirges due in sad array
Slow thro' the church-way path we saw him borne;—
Approach and read (for thou canst read) the lay,
Graved on the stone beneath yon aged thorn.'

The Epitaph

30

Here rests his head upon the lap of Earth,
A Youth, to Fortune and to Fame unknown:
Fair Science frown'd not on his humble birth,
And Melancholy mark'd him for her own.

31

Large was his bounty, and his soul sincere,
Heav'n did a recompense as largely send:
He gave to Misery (all he had), a tear,
He gained from Heav'n ('twas all he wish'd) a friend.

32

No farther seek his merits to disclose,
Or draw his frailties from their dread abode,
(There they alike in trembling hope repose,)
The bosom of his Father and his God.

CHRISTOPHER SMART

A Song to David

CONTENTS. Invocation, *ver.* 1, 2, 3.—The excellence and lustre of David's character in twelve points of view, *ver.* 4; proved from the history of his life, to *ver.* 17.—He consecrates his genius for consolation and edification.—The subjects he made choice of—the Supreme Being—angels; men of renown; the works of nature in all directions, either particularly or collectively considered, to *ver.* 27.—He obtains power over infernal spirits, and the malignity of his enemies; wins the heart of Michal, to *ver.* 30.—Shews that the pillars of knowledge are the monuments of God's works in the first week, to *ver.* 38.—An exercise upon the decalogue, from *ver.* 40 to 49.—The transcendent virtue of praise and adoration, *ver.* 50 and 51.—An exercise upon the seasons, and the right use of them, *ver.* 52 to 64.—An exercise upon the senses, and how to subdue them, from *ver.* 65 to 71.—An amplification in five degrees, which is wrought up to this conclusion, That the best poet who ever lived was thought worthy of the highest honour which possibly can be conceived, *as the Saviour of the world was ascribed to his house, and called his son in the body.*

CHRISTOPHER SMART.

I

O THOU, that sit'st upon a throne,
With harp of high majestic tone,
   To praise the King of kings,
And voice of heaven-ascending swell,
Which, while its deeper notes excell,
   Clear, as a clarion, rings:

To bless each valley, grove, and coast,
And charm the cherub to the post
   Of gratitude in throngs;
To keep the days on Zion's Mount
And send the year to his account
   With dances and with songs:

3

O Servant of God's holiest charge,
The minister of praise at large,
   Which thou mayst now receive,
From thy blest mansion hail and hear,
From topmost eminence appear
   To this the wreath I weave.

4

Great, valiant, pious, good, and clean,
Sublime, contemplative, serene,
   Strong, constant, pleasant, wise!
Bright effluence of exceeding grace;
Best man!—the swiftness and the race,
   The peril, and the prize!

5

Great—from the lustre of his crown,
From Samuel's horn, and God's renown
   Which is the people's voice:
For all the host, from rear to van,
Applauded and embraced the man—
   The man of God's own choice.

6

Valiant—the word, and up he rose—
The fight—he triumphed o'er the foes
   Whom God's just laws abhor;
And, arm'd in gallant faith, he took
Against the boaster, from the brook
   The weapons of the war.

7

Pious—magnificent and grand:
'Twas he the famous temple plann'd
   (The seraph in his soul):
Foremost to give the Lord his dues,
Foremost to bless the welcome news,
   And foremost to condole.

8

Good—from Jehudah's genuine vein,
From God's best nature good in grain,
   His aspect and his heart;
To pity, to forgive, to save,
Witness En-gedi's conscious cave,
   And Shimei's blunted dart.

9

Clean—if perpetual prayer be pure,
And love, which could itself inure
   To fasting and to fear—
Clean in his gestures, hands, and feet,
To smite the lyre, the dance compleat,
   To play the sword and spear.

10

Sublime—invention ever young,
Of vast conception, tow'ring tongue,
   To God the eternal theme;
Notes from yon exaltations caught,
Unrival'd royalty of thought,
   O'er meaner strains supreme.

11

Contemplative—on God to fix
His musings, and above the six
   The sabbath-day he blest:
'Twas then his thoughts self-conquest prun'd,
And heavenly melancholy tun'd
   To bless and bear the rest.

12

Serene—to sow the seeds of peace,
Rememb'ring, when he watch'd the fleece,
   How sweetly Kidron purl'd—
To further knowledge, silence vice,
And plant perpetual paradise
   When God had calmed the world.

13

Strong—in the Lord, who could defy
Satan, and all his powers that lie
   In sempiternal night;
And hell, and horror, and despair
Were as the lion and the bear
   To his undaunted might.

Constant—in love to God THE TRUTH---
Age, manhood, infancy, and youth;
  To Jonathan his friend
Constant, beyond the verge of death;
And Ziba and Mephibosheth
  His endless fame attend.

Pleasant—and various as the year:
Man, soul, and angel, without peer,
  Priest, champion, sage and boy;
In armour or in ephod clad,
His pomp, his piety was glad;
  Majestic was his joy.

Wise—in recovery from his fall,
Whence rose his eminence o'er all,
  Of all the most revil'd;
The light of Israel in his ways,
Wise are his precepts, prayer and praise,
  And counsel to his child.

His muse, bright angel of his verse,
Gives balm for all the thorns that pierce,
  For all the pangs that rage;
Blest light, still gaining on the gloom,
The more than Michal of his bloom,
  Th' Abishag of his age.

He sung of God—the mighty source
Of all things—the stupendous force
  On which all strength depends;
From whose right arm, beneath whose eyes,
All period, pow'r, and enterprize
  Commences, reigns, and ends.

19

Angels—their ministry and meed,
Which to and fro with blessings speed,
  Or with their citterns wait;
Where Michael with his millions bows,
Where dwells the seraph and his spouse,
  The cherub and her mate.

20

Of man—the semblance and effect
Of God and Love—the saint elect
  For infinite applause—
To rule the land, and briny broad,
To be laborious in his laud,
  And heroes in his cause.

21

The world—the clust'ring spheres he made,
The glorious light, the soothing shade,
  Dale, champaign, grove, and hill;
The multitudinous abyss,
Where secrecy remains in bliss
  And wisdom hides her skill.

22

Trees, plants, and flow'rs—of virtuous root:
Gem yielding blossom, yielding fruit,
   Choice gums and precious balm;
Bless ye the nosegay in the vale,
And with the sweetners of the gale
   Enrich the thankful psalm.

23

Of fowl—e'en ev'ry beak and wing
Which chear the winter, hail the spring,
   That live in peace or prey;
They that make music, or that mock,
The quail, the brave domestic cock,
   The raven, swan, and jay.

24

Of fishes—ev'ry size and shape,
Which nature frames of light escape,
   Devouring man to shun:
The shells are in the wealthy deep,
The shoals upon the surface leap
   And love the glancing sun.

25

Of beasts—the beaver plods his task;
While the sleek tigers roll and bask,
   Nor yet the shades arouse;
Her cave the mining coney scoops;
Where o'er the mead the mountain stoops
   The kids exult and brouse.

Of gems—their virtue and their price,
Which hid in earth from man's device,
   Their darts of lustre sheathe:
The jasper of the master's stamp,
The topaz blazing like a lamp
   Among the mines beneath.

Blest was the tenderness he felt
When to his graceful harp he knelt,
   And did for audience call;
When Satan with his hand he quell'd,
And in serene suspence he held
   The frantic throes of Saul.

His furious foes no more malign'd
As he such melody divin'd,
   And sense and soul detain'd;
Now striking strong, now soothing soft,
He sent the godly sounds aloft,
   Or in delight refrain'd.

When up to heaven his thoughts he pil'd
From fervent lips fair Michal smil'd,
   As blush to blush she stood;
And chose herself the queen, and gave
Her utmost from her heart, 'So brave,
   And plays his hymns so good.'

The pillars of the Lord are seven,
Which stand from earth to topmost heav'n;
  His wisdom drew the plan;
His WORD accomplished the design,
From brightest gem to deepest mine,
  From CHRIST enthron'd to man.

Alpha, the cause of causes, first
In station—fountain, whence the burst
  Of light, and blaze of day;
Whence bold attempt, and brave advance,
Have motion, life, and ordinance,
  And heaven itself its stay.

Gamma supports the glorious arch
On which angelic legions march,
  And is with sapphires pav'd;
Thence the fleet clouds are sent adrift,
And thence the painted folds, that lift
  The crimson veil, are wav'd.

Eta with living sculpture breathes,
With verdant carvings, flow'ry wreaths,
  Of never-wasting bloom;
In strong relief his goodly base
All instruments of labour grace,
  The trowel, spade, and loom.

Next Theta stands to the Supreme—
Who formed, in number, sign, and scheme,
  Th' illustrious lights that are;
And one address'd his saffron robe,
And one, clad in a silver globe,
  Held rule with ev'ry star.

Iota's tuned to choral hymns
Of those that fly, while he that swims
  In thankful safety lurks;
And foot, and chapitre, and niche
The various histories enrich
  Of God's recorded works.

Sigma presents the social droves
With him that solitary roves,
  And man of all the chief;
Fair on whose face, and stately frame,
Did God impress his hallow'd name,
  For ocular belief.

OMEGA! GREATEST and the BEST,
Stands sacred to the day of rest,
  For gratitude and thought;
Which blessed the world upon his pole,
And gave the universe his goal,
  And clos'd th' infernal draught.

O DAVID, scholar of the Lord!
Such is thy science, whence reward
   And infinite degree;
O strength, O sweetness, lasting ripe!
God's harp thy symbol, and thy type
   The lion and the bee!

39

There is but One who ne'er rebell'd,
But One by passion unimpell'd,
   By pleasures unintice't;
He from himself his semblance sent,
Grand object of his own content,
   And saw the God in CHRIST.

40

Tell them, I am, JEHOVA said
To MOSES; while earth heard in dread,
   And, smitten to the heart,
At once above, beneath, around,
All Nature, without voice or sound,
   Replied, 'O LORD, THOU ART.'

41

Thou art—to give and to confirm,
For each his talent and his term;
   All flesh thy bounties share.
Thou shalt not call thy brother fool;
The porches of the Christian school
   Are meekness, peace, and pray'r.

Open, and naked of offence,
Man's made of mercy, soul, and sense
  (God armed the snail and wilk);
Be good to him that pulls thy plough;
Due food and care, due rest, allow
  For her that yields thee milk.

43

Rise up before the hoary head,
And God's benign commandment dread,
  Which says thou shalt not die;
'Not as I will, but as Thou wilt',
Prayed He whose conscience knew no guilt;
  With Whose bless'd pattern vie.

44

Use all thy passions!—love is thine,
And joy, and jealousy divine,
  Thine hope's eternal fort;
And care thy leisure to disturb,
With fear concupiscence to curb,
  And rapture to transport.

45

Act simply, as occasion asks;
Put mellow wine in season'd casks;
  Till not with ass and bull;
Remember thy baptismal bond;
Keep from commixtures foul and fond,
  Nor work thy flax with wool.

Distribute: pay the Lord his tithe,
And make the widow's heart-strings blithe;
　　Resort with those that weep:
As you from all and each expect,
For all and each thy love direct,
　　And render as you reap.

The slander and its bearer spurn,
And, propagating praise, sojourn
　　To make thy welcome last;
Turn from Old Adam to the New;
By hope futurity pursue;
　　Look upwards to the past.

Controul thine eye: salute success,
Honour the wiser, happier bless,
　　And for thy neighbour feel;
Grutch not of mammon and his leaven,
Work emulation up to heaven
　　By knowledge and by zeal.

O DAVID, highest in the list
Of worthies, on God's ways insist,
　　The genuine word repeat:
Vain are the documents of men,
And vain the flourish of the pen
　　That keeps the fool's conceit.

50

PRAISE above all—for praise prevails:
Heap up the measure, load the scales,
    And good to goodness add;
The generous soul her saviour aids,
But peevish obloquy degrades;
    The Lord is great and glad.

51

For ADORATION all the ranks
Of angels yield eternal thanks,
    And DAVID in the midst;
With God's good poor which, last and least
In man's esteem, thou to thy feast,
    O blessed bridegroom, bidst.

52

For ADORATION seasons change,
And order, truth, and beauty range,
    Adjust, attract, and fill:
The grass the polyanthus cheques;
And polish'd porphyry reflects,
    By the descending rill.

53

Rich almonds colour to the prime
For ADORATION; tendrils climb,
    And fruit-trees pledge their gems;
And Ivis, with her gorgeous vest,
Builds for her eggs her cunning nest,
    And bell-flowers bow their stems.

With vinous syrup cedars spout;
From rocks pure honey gushing out
　　For ADORATION springs;
All scenes of painting croud the map
Of nature; to the mermaid's pap
　　The scalèd infant clings.

The spotted ounce and playsome cubs
Run rustling 'mongst the flow'ring shrubs,
　　And lizards feed the moss;
For ADORATION beasts embark,
While waves upholding halcyon's ark
　　No longer roar and toss.

While Israel sits beneath his fig,
With coral root and amber sprig
　　The wean'd advent'rer sports;
Where to the palm the jasmin cleaves,
For ADORATION 'mongst the leaves
　　The gale his peace reports.

Increasing days their reign exalt,
Nor in the pink and mottled vault
　　The opposing spirits tilt;
And, by the coasting reader spied,
The silverlings and crusions glide
　　For ADORATION gilt.

For ADORATION rip'ning canes,
And cocoa's purest milk detains
　　The western pilgrim's staff;
Where rain in clasping boughs inclos'd,
And vines with oranges dispos'd,
　　Embow'r the social laugh.

Now labour his reward receives,
For ADORATION counts his sheaves
　　To Peace, her bounteous prince;
The nectarine his strong tint imbibes,
And apples of ten thousand tribes,
　　And quick peculiar quince.

The wealthy crops of whit'ning rice,
'Mongst thyine woods and groves of spice,
　　For ADORATION grow;
And, marshall'd in the fencèd land,
The peaches and pomegranates stand,
　　Where wild carnations blow.

The laurels with the winter strive;
The crocus burnishes alive
　　Upon the snow-clad earth;
For ADORATION myrtles stay
To keep the garden from dismay,
　　And bless the sight from dearth.

The pheasant shows his pompous neck;
And ermine, jealous of a speck,
   With fear eludes offence;
The sable, with his glossy pride,
For ADORATION is descried
   Where frosts the wave condense.

The chearful holly, pensive yew,
And holy thorn, their trim renew;
   The squirrel hoards his nuts:
All creatures batten o'er their stores,
And careful nature all her doors
   For ADORATION shuts.

For ADORATION, DAVID's psalms
Lift up the heart to deeds of alms;
   And he, who kneels and chants,
Prevails his passions to controul,
Finds meat and med'cine to the soul,
   Which for translation pants.

For ADORATION, beyond match
The scholar bulfinch aims to catch
   The soft flute's iv'ry touch;
And, careless on the hazel spray,
The daring redbreast keeps at bay
   The damsel's greedy clutch.

66

For ADORATION, in the skies
The Lord's philosopher espies
 The Dog, the Ram, and Rose;
The planet's ring, Orion's sword;
Nor is his greatness less ador'd
 In the vile worm that glows.

67

For ADORATION, on the strings
The western breezes work their wings
 The captive ear to sooth.
Hark! 'tis a voice—how still, and small—
That makes the cataracts to fall,
 Or bids the sea be smooth.

68

For ADORATION, incense comes
From bezoar, and Arabian gums,
 And from the civet's furr:
But as for prayer, or e're it faints,
Far better is the breath of saints
 Than galbanum or myrrh.

69

For ADORATION, from the down
Of dam'sins to th' anana's crown,
 God sends to tempt the taste;
And while the luscious zest invites,
The sense, that in the scene delights,
 Commands desire be chaste.

For ADORATION, all the paths
Of grace are open, all the baths
   Of purity refresh;
And all the rays of glory beam
To deck the man of God's esteem
   Who triumphs o'er the flesh.

71

For ADORATION, in the dome
Of CHRIST, the sparrows find an home,
   And on his olives perch;
The swallow also dwells with thee,
O man of God's humility,
   Within his Saviour's CHURCH.

72

Sweet is the dew that falls betimes
And drops upon the leafy limes;
   Sweet, Hermon's fragrant air:
Sweet is the lilly's silver bell,
And sweet the wakeful tapers smell
   That watch for early pray'r.

73

Sweet the young nurse, with love intense,
Which smiles o'er sleeping innocence;
   Sweet when the lost arrive;
Sweet the musician's ardour beats,
While his vague mind's in quest of sweets,
   The choicest flow'rs to hive.

Sweeter, in all the strains of love,
The language of thy turtle dove,
  Pair'd to thy swelling chord;
Sweeter, with every grace endu'd,
The glory of thy gratitude
  Respir'd unto the Lord.

Strong is the horse upon his speed;
Strong in pursuit the rapid glede
  Which makes at once his game;
Strong the tall ostrich on the ground;
Strong through the turbulent profound
  Shoots xiphias to his aim.

Strong is the lion—like a coal
His eyeball, like a bastion's mole
  His chest against the foes;
Strong, the gier-eagle on his sail,
Strong against tide, th' enormous whale
  Emerges, as he goes.

But stronger still, in earth and air
And in the sea, the man of pray'r,
  And far beneath the tide;
And in the seat to faith assign'd,
Where ask is have, where seek is find,
  Where knock is open wide.

Beauteous the fleet before the gale;
Beauteous the multitudes in mail,
    Ranked arms and crested heads;
Beauteous the garden's umbrage mild,
Walk, water, meditated wild,
    And all the bloomy beds.

Beauteous the moon full on the lawn;
And beauteous, when the veil's withdrawn,
    The virgin to her spouse;
Beauteous the temple, deck'd and fill'd,
When to the heav'n of heav'ns they build
    Their heart-directed vows.

Beauteous, yea beauteous more than these,
The shepherd king upon his knees,
    For his momentous trust;
With wish of infinite conceit,
For man, beast, mute, the small and great,
    And prostrate dust to dust.

Precious the bounteous widow's mite;
And precious, for extream delight,
    The largess from the churl;
Precious the ruby's blushing blaze,
And alba's blest imperial rays,
    And pure cerulean pearl.

Precious the penitential tear;
And precious is the sigh sincere,
   Acceptable to God;
And precious are the winning flow'rs,
In gladsome Israel's feast of bow'rs,
   Bound on the hallow'd sod.

83

More precious that diviner part
Of David, even the Lord's own heart,
   Great, beautiful, and new;
In all things where it was intent,
In all extreams, in each event,
   Proof—answ'ring true to true.

84

Glorious the sun in mid career;
Glorious th' assembled fires appear;
   Glorious the comet's train;
Glorious the trumpet and alarm;
Glorious th' almighty stretched-out arm;
   Glorious th' enraptur'd main;

85

Glorious the northern lights a-stream;
Glorious the song, when God's the theme;
   Glorious the thunder's roar;
Glorious hosannah from the den,
Glorious the catholic amen;
   Glorious the martyr's gore.

Glorious—more glorious, is the crown
Of Him that brought salvation down,
    By meekness, called thy Son:
Thou at stupendous truth believ'd;—
And now the matchless deed's atchiev'd,
    DETERMINED, DARED, and DONE.

OLIVER GOLDSMITH

The Deserted Village

SWEET AUBURN! loveliest village of the plain,
Where health and plenty cheer'd the labouring swain,
Where smiling spring its earliest visit paid,
And parting summer's lingering blooms delay'd:
Dear lovely bowers of innocence and ease,   5
Seats of my youth, when every sport could please,
How often have I loiter'd o'er thy green,
Where humble happiness endear'd each scene;
How often have I paus'd on every charm,
The shelter'd cot, the cultivated farm,   10
The never failing brook, the busy mill,
The decent church that topp'd the neighbouring hill,
The hawthorn bush, with seats beneath the shade,
For talking age and whispering lovers made;
How often have I bless'd the coming day,   15
When toil remitting lent its turn to play,
And all the village train, from labour free,
Led up their sports beneath the spreading tree;
While many a pastime circled in the shade,
The young contending as the old survey'd;   20
And many a gambol frolick'd o'er the ground,
And sleights of art and feats of strength went round;
And still as each repeated pleasure tir'd,
Succeeding sports the mirthful band inspir'd;
The dancing pair that simply sought renown,   25
By holding out to tire each other down;

The swain mistrustless of his smutted face,
While secret laughter titter'd round the place;
The bashful virgin's sidelong looks of love,
The matron's glance that would those looks reprove.   30
These were thy charms, sweet village; sports like these,
With sweet succession taught e'en toil to please;
These round thy bowers their cheerful influence shed,
These were thy charms—But all these charms are fled.

  Sweet smiling village, loveliest of the lawn,   35
Thy sports are fled, and all thy charms withdrawn;
Amidst thy bowers the tyrant's hand is seen,
And desolation saddens all thy green:
One only master grasps the whole domain,
And half a tillage stints thy smiling plain :   40
No more thy glassy brook reflects the day,
But choked with sedges works its weedy way;
Along thy glades, a solitary guest,
The hollow-sounding bittern guards its nest;
Amidst thy desert walks the lapwing flies,   45
And tires their echoes with unvaried cries.
Sunk are thy bowers in shapeless ruin all,
And the long grass o'ertops the mouldering wall;
And, trembling, shrinking from the spoiler's hand,
Far, far away thy children leave the land.   50

  Ill fares the land, to hastening ills a prey,
Where wealth accumulates, and men decay:
Princes and lords may flourish, or may fade;
A breath can make them, as a breath has made;
But a bold peasantry, their country's pride,   55
When once destroy'd, can never be supplied.

  A time there was, ere England's griefs began,
When every rood of ground maintain'd its man;
For him light labour spread her wholesome store,
Just gave what life requir'd, but gave no more: 60
His best companions, innocence and health;

And his best riches, ignorance of wealth.

But times are alter'd; trade's unfeeling train
Usurp the land, and dispossess the swain;
Along the lawn, where scatter'd hamlets rose,   65
Unwieldy wealth, and cumbrous pomp repose;
And every want to luxury allied,
And every pang that folly pays to pride.
Those gentle hours that plenty bade to bloom,
Those calm desires that ask'd but little room,   70
Those healthful sports that grac'd the peaceful scene,
Liv'd in each look, and brighten'd all the green;
These, far departing, seek a kinder shore,
And rural mirth and manners are no more.

Sweet AUBURN! parent of the blissful hour,   75
Thy glades forlorn confess the tyrant's power.
Here, as I take my solitary rounds,
Amidst thy tangling walks, and ruin'd grounds,
And, many a year elaps'd, return to view
Where once the cottage stood, the hawthorn grew,   80
Remembrance wakes with all her busy train,
Swells at my breast, and turns the past to pain.

In all my wanderings round this world of care,
In all my griefs—and God has given my share—
I still had hopes my latest hours to crown,   85
Amidst these humble bowers to lay me down;
To husband out life's taper at the close,
And keep the flame from wasting by repose.
I still had hopes, for pride attends us still,
Amidst the swains to show my book-learn'd skill,   90
Around my fire an evening group to draw,
And tell of all I felt, and all I saw;
And as an hare, whom hounds and horns pursue,
Pants to the place from whence at first she flew,
I still had hopes, my long vexations pass'd,   95
Here to return—and die at home at last.

O bless'd retirement, friend to life's decline,
Retreats from care, that never must be mine,
How happy he who crowns, in shades like these,
A youth of labour with an age of ease;   100
Who quits a world where strong temptations try,
And, since 'tis hard to combat, learns to fly!
For him no wretches, born to work and weep,
Explore the mine, or tempt the dangerous deep;
No surly porter stands in guilty state   105
To spurn imploring famine from the gate;
But on he moves to meet his latter end,
Angels around befriending Virtue's friend;
Bends to the grave with unperceiv'd decay,
While Resignation gently slopes the way;   110
And, all his prospects brightening to the last,
His Heaven commences ere the world be pass'd!
    Sweet was the sound, when oft at evening's close
Up yonder hill the village murmur rose;
There, as I pass'd with careless steps and slow,   115
The mingling notes came soften'd from below;
The swain responsive as the milkmaid sung,
The sober herd that low'd to meet their young;
The noisy geese that gabbled o'er the pool,
The playful children just let loose from school;   120
The watch-dog's voice that bay'd the whisp'ring wind,
And the loud laugh that spoke the vacant mind;
These all in sweet confusion sought the shade,
And fill'd each pause the nightingale had made.
But now the sounds of population fail,   125
No cheerful murmurs fluctuate in the gale,
No busy steps the grass-grown footway tread,
But all the blooming flush of life is fled.
All but yon widow'd, solitary thing,
That feebly bends beside the plashy spring;   130
She, wretched matron, forc'd, in age, for bread,

To strip the brook with mantling cresses spread,
To pick her wintry faggot from the thorn,
To seek her nightly shed, and weep till morn;
She only left of all the harmless train,   135
The sad historian of the pensive plain.

  Near yonder copse, where once the garden smil'd,
And still where many a garden flower grows wild;
There, where a few torn shrubs the place disclose,
The village preacher's modest mansion rose.   140
A man he was to all the country dear,
And passing rich with forty pounds a year;
Remote from towns he ran his godly race,
Nor e'er had chang'd, nor wish'd to change his place;
Unpractis'd he to fawn, or seek for power,   145
By doctrines fashion'd to the varying hour;
Far other aims his heart had learn'd to prize,
More skill'd to raise the wretched than to rise.
His house was known to all the vagrant train,
He chid their wanderings, but reliev'd their pain;   150
The long remember'd beggar was his guest,
Whose beard descending swept his aged breast;
The ruin'd spendthrift, now no longer proud,
Claim'd kindred there, and had his claims allow'd;
The broken soldier, kindly bade to stay,   155
Sat by his fire, and talk'd the night away;
Wept o'er his wounds, or, tales of sorrow done,
Shoulder'd his crutch, and show'd how fields were won.
Pleas'd with his guests, the good man learn'd to glow,
And quite forgot their vices in their woe;   160
Careless their merits, or their faults to scan,
His pity gave ere charity began.

  Thus to relieve the wretched was his pride,
And e'en his failings lean'd to Virtue's side;
But in his duty prompt at every call,   165
He watch'd and wept, he pray'd and felt, for all:

And, as a bird each fond endearment tries
To tempt its new-fledged offspring to the skies,
He tried each art, reprov'd each dull delay,
Allur'd to brighter worlds, and led the way.   170
  Beside the bed where parting life was laid,
And sorrow, guilt, and pain by turns dismay'd,
The reverend champion stood. At his control
Despair and anguish fled the struggling soul;
Comfort came down the trembling wretch to raise,   175
And his last faltering accents whisper'd praise.
  At church, with meek and unaffected grace,
His looks adorn'd the venerable place;
Truth from his lips prevail'd with double sway,
And fools, who came to scoff, remain'd to pray.   180
The service pass'd, around the pious man,
With steady zeal, each honest rustic ran;
E'en children follow'd, with endearing wile,
And pluck'd his gown, to share the good man's smile.
His ready smile a parent's warmth express'd,   185
Their welfare pleas'd him, and their cares distress'd;
To them his heart, his love, his griefs were given,
But all his serious thoughts had rest in Heaven.
As some tall cliff, that lifts its awful form,
Swells from the vale, and midway leaves the storm,   190
Though round its breast the rolling clouds are spread,
Eternal sunshine settles on its head.
  Beside yon straggling fence that skirts the way
With blossom'd furze, unprofitably gay,
There, in his noisy mansion, skill'd to rule,   195
The village master taught his little school;
A man severe he was, and stern to view;
I knew him well, and every truant knew;
Well had the boding tremblers learn'd to trace
The day's disasters in his morning face;   200
Full well they laugh'd, with counterfeited glee,

At all his jokes, for many a joke had he;
Full well the busy whisper, circling round,
Convey'd the dismal tidings when he frown'd;
Yet he was kind; or if severe in aught,   205
The love he bore to learning was in fault;
The village all declared how much he knew;
'Twas certain he could write, and cipher too;
Lands he could measure, terms and tides presage,
And e'en the story ran that he could gauge.   210
In arguing too, the parson own'd his skill,
For e'en though vanquish'd, he could argue still;
While words of learned length and thundering sound
Amazed the gazing rustics rang'd around;
And still they gazed, and still the wonder grew   215
That one small head could carry all he knew.
   But pass'd is all his fame. The very spot
Where many a time he triumph'd, is forgot.
Near yonder thorn, that lifts its head on high,
Where once the signpost caught the passing eye,   220
Low lies that house where nutbrown draughts inspir'd,
Where graybeard mirth and smiling toil retir'd,
Where village statesmen talk'd with looks profound,
And news much older than their ale went round.
Imagination fondly stoops to trace   225
The parlour splendours of that festive place;
The whitewash'd wall, the nicely sanded floor,
The varnish'd clock that click'd behind the door:
The chest contriv'd a double debt to pay,
A bed by night, a chest of drawers by day;   230
The pictures plac'd for ornament and use,
The twelve good rules, the royal game of goose;
The hearth, except when winter chill'd the day,
With aspen boughs, and flowers, and fennel gay;
While broken teacups, wisely kept for show,   235
Rang'd o'er the chimney, glisten'd in a row.

Vain transitory splendours! could not all
Reprieve the tottering mansion from its fall?
Obscure it sinks, nor shall it more impart
An hour's importance to the poor man's heart;   240
Thither no more the peasant shall repair
To sweet oblivion of his daily care;
No more the farmer's news, the barber's tale,
No more the woodman's ballad shall prevail;
No more the smith his dusky brow shall clear,   245
Relax his ponderous strength, and lean to hear;
The host himself no longer shall be found
Careful to see the mantling bliss go round;
Nor the coy maid, half willing to be press'd,
Shall kiss the cup to pass it to the rest.   250
    Yes! let the rich deride, the proud disdain,
These simple blessings of the lowly train;
To me more dear, congenial to my heart,
One native charm, than all the gloss of art;
Spontaneous joys, where Nature has its play,   255
The soul adopts, and owns their firstborn sway;
Lightly they frolic o'er the vacant mind,
Unenvied, unmolested, unconfin'd:
But the long pomp, the midnight masquerade,
With all the freaks of wanton wealth array'd,   260
In these, ere triflers half their wish obtain,
The toiling pleasure sickens into pain;
And, e'en while fashion's brightest arts decoy,
The heart distrusting asks, if this be joy.
    Ye friends to truth, ye statesmen, who survey   265
The rich man's joys increase, the poor's decay,
'Tis yours to judge, how wide the limits stand
Between a splendid and a happy land.
Proud swells the tide with loads of freighted ore,
And shouting Folly hails them from her shore;   270
Hoards e'en beyond the miser's wish abound,

And rich men flock from all the world around.
Yet count our gains. This wealth is but a name
That leaves our useful products still the same.
Not so the loss. The man of wealth and pride   275
Takes up a space that many poor supplied;
Space for his lake, his park's extended bounds,
Space for his horses, equipage, and hounds;
The robe that wraps his limbs in silken sloth
Has robb'd the neighbouring fields of half their growth; 280
His seat, where solitary sports are seen,
Indignant spurns the cottage from the green;
Around the world each needful product flies,
For all the luxuries the world supplies:
Whilst thus the land, adorn'd for pleasure all,   285
In barren splendour feebly waits the fall.
    As some fair female, unadorn'd and plain,
Secure to please while youth confirms her reign,
Slights every borrow'd charm that dress supplies,
Nor shares with art the triumph of her eyes: 290
But when those charms are pass'd, for charms are frail,
When time advances, and when lovers fail,
She then shines forth, solicitous to bless,
In all the glaring impotence of dress.
Thus fares the land, by luxury betray'd,   295
In nature's simplest charms at first array'd,
But verging to decline, its splendours rise,
Its vistas strike, its palaces surprise;
While, scourg'd by famine, from the smiling land
The mournful peasant leads his humble band;   300
And while he sinks, without one arm to save,
The country blooms—a garden, and a grave.
    Where then, ah! where, shall poverty reside,
To 'scape the pressure of contiguous pride?
If to some common's fenceless limits stray'd,   305
He drives his flock to pick the scanty blade,

62

Those fenceless fields the sons of wealth divide,
And e'en the bare-worn common is denied.
 If to the city sped—What waits him there?
To see profusion that he must not share;   310
To see ten thousand baneful arts combin'd
To pamper luxury, and thin mankind;
To see those joys the sons of pleasure know,
Extorted from his fellow-creatures' woe.
Here, while the courtier glitters in brocade,   315
There the pale artist plies the sickly trade;
Here, while the proud their long-drawn pomps display,
There the black gibbet glooms beside the way.
The dome where Pleasure holds her midnight reign
Here, richly deck'd, admits the gorgeous train;   320
Tumultous grandeur crowds the blazing square,
The rattling chariots clash, the torches glare.
Sure scenes like these no troubles e'er annoy!
Sure these denote one universal joy!
Are these thy serious thoughts?—Ah, turn thine eyes 325
Where the poor houseless shivering female lies.
She once, perhaps, in village plenty bless'd,
Has wept at tales of innocence distress'd;
Her modest looks the cottage might adorn,
Sweet as the primrose peeps beneath the thorn;   330
Now lost to all; her friends, her virtue fled,
Near her betrayer's door she lays her head,
And, pinch'd with cold, and shrinking from the shower,
With heavy heart deplores that luckless hour,
When idly first, ambitious of the town,   335
She left her wheel and robes of country brown.
 Do thine, sweet AUBURN, thine, the loveliest train,
Do thy fair tribes participate her pain?
E'en now, perhaps, by cold and hunger led,
At proud men's doors they ask a little bread!   340
 Ah, no. To distant climes, a dreary scene,

Where half the convex world intrudes between,
Through torrid tracts with fainting steps they go,
Where wild Altama murmurs to their woe.
Far different there from all that charm'd before,   345
The various terrors of that horrid shore;
Those blazing suns that dart a downward ray,
And fiercely shed intolerable day;
Those matted woods where birds forget to sing,
But silent bats in drowsy clusters cling;   350
Those poisonous fields with rank luxuriance crown'd,
Where the dark scorpion gathers death around:
Where at each step the stranger fears to wake
The rattling terrors of the vengeful snake;
Where crouching tigers wait their hapless prey;   355
And savage men more murderous still than they;
While oft in whirls the mad tornado flies,
Mingling the ravag'd landscape with the skies.
Far different these from every former scene,
The cooling brook, the grassy-vested green,   360
The breezy covert of the warbling grove,
That only shelter'd thefts of harmless love.
   Good Heaven! what sorrows gloom'd that parting day,
That call'd them from their native walks away;
When the poor exiles, every pleasure pass'd,   365
Hung round the bowers, and fondly look'd their last,
And took a long farewell, and wish'd in vain
For seats like these beyond the western main;
And, shuddering still to face the distant deep,
Return'd and wept, and still return'd to weep.   370
The good old sire the first prepar'd to go
To new-found worlds, and wept for others' woe;
But for himself, in conscious virtue brave,
He only wish'd for worlds beyond the grave.
His lovely daughter, lovelier in her tears,   375
The fond companion of his helpless years,

Silent went next, neglectful of her charms,
And left a lover's for a father's arms.
With louder plaints the mother spoke her woes,
And bless'd the cot where every pleasure rose;   380
And kiss'd her thoughtless babes with many a tear,
And clasp'd them close, in sorrow doubly dear;
Whilst her fond husband strove to lend relief
In all the silent manliness of grief.

O luxury! thou cursed by Heaven's decree,   385
How ill exchang'd are things like these for thee!
How do thy potions, with insidious joy,
Diffuse their pleasures only to destroy!
Kingdoms by thee, to sickly greatness grown,
Boast of a florid vigour not their own: 390
At every draught more large and large they grow,
A bloated mass of rank unwieldy woe;
Till sapp'd their strength, and every part unsound,
Down, down they sink, and spread a ruin round.

E'en now the devastation is begun,   395
And half the business of destruction done;
E'en now, methinks, as pondering here I stand,
I see the rural virtues leave the land:
Down where yon anchoring vessel spreads the sail,
That idly waiting flaps with every gale,   400
Downward they move, a melancholy band,
Pass from the shore, and darken all the strand.
Contented toil, and hospitable care,
And kind connubial tenderness, are there;
And piety with wishes plac'd above,   405
And steady loyalty, and faithful love.
And thou, sweet Poetry, thou loveliest maid,
Still first to fly where sensual joys invade;
Unfit in these degenerate times of shame,
To catch the heart, or strike for honest fame;   410
Dear charming nymph, neglected and decried,

My shame in crowds, my solitary pride;
Thou source of all my bliss, and all my woe,
That found'st me poor at first, and keep'st me so;
Thou guide by which the nobler arts excel,   415
Thou nurse of every virtue, fare thee well!
Farewell! And oh! where'er thy voice be tried,
On Torno's cliffs, or Pambamarca's side,
Whether where equinoctial fervours glow,
Or winter wraps the polar world in snow,   420
Still let thy voice, prevailing over time,
Redress the rigours of th' inclement clime;
Aid slighted Truth; with thy persuasive train
Teach erring man to spurn the rage of gain;
Teach him, that states of native strength possess'd,   425
Though very poor, may still be very bless'd;
That trade's proud empire hastes to swift decay,
As ocean sweeps the labour'd mole away;
While self-dependent power can time defy,
As rocks resist the billows and the sky.   430

Retaliation

Of old, when Scarron his companions invited,
Each guest brought his dish, and the feast was united;
If our landlord supplies us with beef and with fish,
Let each guest bring himself, and he brings the best dish:
Our Dean shall be venison, just fresh from the plains;   5
Our Burke shall be tongue, with the garnish of brains;
Our Will shall be wild fowl, of excellent flavour,
And Dick with his pepper, shall heighten their savour:
Our Cumberland's sweetbread its place shall obtain,
And Douglas is pudding, substantial and plain: 10
Our Garrick's a salad; for in him we see

Oil, vinegar, sugar, and saltness agree:
To make out the dinner full certain I am,
That Ridge is anchovy, and Reynolds is lamb;
That Hickey's a capon, and by the same rule,   15
Magnanimous Goldsmith a gooseberry fool.
At a dinner so various, at such a repast,
Who'd not be a glutton, and stick to the last?
Here, waiter! more wine, let me sit while I'm able,
Till all my companions sink under the table;   20
Then, with chaos and blunders encircling my head,
Let me ponder, and tell what I think of the dead.

   Here lies the good Dean, reunited to earth,
Who mix'd reason with pleasure, and wisdom with mirth:
If he had any faults, he has left us in doubt,   25
At least, in six weeks I could not find 'em out;
Yet some have declared, and it can't be denied 'em,
That sly-boots was cursedly cunning to hide 'em.

   Here lies our good Edmund, whose genius was such,
We scarcely can praise it, or blame it too much;   30
Who, born for the Universe, narrow'd his mind,
And to party gave up what was meant for mankind:
Tho' fraught with all learning, yet straining his throat
To persuade Tommy Townshend to lend him a vote;
Who, too deep for his hearers, still went on refining,   35
And thought of convincing, while they thought of dining;
Though equal to all things, for all things unfit,
Too nice for a statesman, too proud for a wit:
For a patriot, too cool; for a drudge, disobedient;
And too fond of the *right* to pursue the *expedient*.   40
In short, 'twas his fate, unemploy'd, or in place, sir,
To eat mutton cold, and cut blocks with a razor.

   Here lies honest William, whose heart was a mint,
While the owner ne'er knew half the good that was in't;
The pupil of impulse, it forc'd him along,   45
His conduct still right, with his argument wrong;

Still aiming at honour, yet fearing to roam,
The coachman was tipsy, the chariot drove home;
Would you ask for his merits? alas! he had none;
What was good was spontaneous, his faults were his own. 50
Here lies honest Richard, whose fate I must sigh at;
Alas! that such frolic should now be so quiet!
What spirits were his! what wit and what whim!
Now breaking a jest, and now breaking a limb;
Now wrangling and grumbling to keep up the ball; 55
Now teasing and vexing, yet laughing at all!
In short, so provoking a devil was Dick,
That we wish'd him full ten times a day at Old Nick;
But, missing his mirth and agreeable vein,
As often we wish'd to have Dick back again. 60

Here Cumberland lies, having acted his parts,
The Terence of England, the mender of hearts;
A flattering painter, who made it his care
To draw men as they ought to be, not as they are.
His gallants are all faultless, his women divine, 65
And comedy wonders at being so fine;
Like a tragedy queen he has dizen'd her out,
Or rather like tragedy giving a rout.
His fools have their follies so lost in a crowd
Of virtues and feelings, that folly grows proud; 70
And coxcombs, alike in their failings alone,
Adopting his portraits, are pleas'd with their own.
Say, where has our poet this malady caught?
Or wherefore his characters thus without fault?
Say, was it that vainly directing his view 75
To find out men's virtues, and finding them few,
Quite sick of pursuing each troublesome elf,
He grew lazy at last, and drew from himself?

Here Douglas retires, from his toils to relax,
The scourge of imposters, the terror of quacks: 80
Come, all ye quack bards, and ye quacking divines,

Come, and dance on the spot where your tyrant reclines:
When Satire and Censure encircl'd his throne.
I fear'd for your safety, I fear'd for my own;
But now he is gone, and we want a detector,   85
Our Dodds shall be pious, our Kenricks shall lecture;
Macpherson write bombast, and call it a style,
Our Townshend make speeches, and I shall compile;
New Lauders and Bowers the Tweed shall cross over,
No countrymen living their tricks to discover;   90
Detection her taper shall quench to a spark,
And Scotchman meet Scotchman, and cheat in the dark.

   Here lies David Garrick, describe him who can,
An abridgment of all that was pleasant in man;
As an actor, confess'd without rival to shine: 95
As a wit, if not first, in the very first line:
Yet, with talents like these, and an excellent heart,
This man had his failings, a dupe to his art.
Like an ill-judging beauty, his colours he spread,
And be-plaster'd with rouge his own natural red.   100
On the stage he was natural, simple, affecting;
'Twas only that when he was off he was acting.
With no reason on earth to go out of his way,
He turn'd and he varied full ten times a day.
Though secure of our hearts, yet confoundedly sick   105
If they were not his own by finessing and trick:
He cast off his friends, as a huntsman his pack,
For he knew when he pleas'd he could whistle them back.
Of praise a mere glutton, he swallow'd what came,
And the puff of a dunce he mistook it for fame;   110
Till his relish grown callous, almost to disease,
Who pepper'd the highest was surest to please.
But let us be candid, and speak out our mind,
If dunces applauded, he paid them in kind.
Ye Kenricks, ye Kellys, and Woodfalls so grave,   115
What a commerce was yours while you got and you gave!

How did Grub-street re-echo the shouts that you rais'd,
While he was be-Roscius'd, and you were be-prais'd!
But peace to his spirit, wherever it flies,
To act as an angel, and mix with the skies: 120
Those poets, who owe their best fame to his skill,
Shall still be his flatterers, go where he will.
Old Shakespeare receive him, with praise and with love,
And Beaumonts and Bens be his Kellys above.

   Here Hickey reclines, a most blunt pleasant creature, 125
And slander itself must allow him good nature:
He cherish'd his friend, and he relish'd a bumper;
Yet one fault he had, and that was a thumper.
Perhaps you may ask if the man was a miser?
I answer, no, no, for he always was wiser: 130
Too courteous perhaps, or obligingly flat?
His very worst foe can't accuse him of that:
Perhaps he confided in men as they go,
And so was too foolishly honest? Ah no!
Then what was his failing? come, tell it, and burn ye! 135
He was, could he help it? a special attorney.

   Here Reynolds is laid, and, to tell you my mind,
He has not left a better or wiser behind:
His pencil was striking, resistless, and grand;
His manners were gentle, complying, and bland;   140
Still born to improve us in every part,
His pencil our faces, his manners our heart:
To coxcombs averse, yet most civilly steering,
When they judg'd without skill he was still hard of hearing;
When they talk'd of their Raphaels, Coreggios, and stuff, 145
He shifted his trumpet, and only took snuff.

JOHN LANGHORNE

The Country Justice

A poem in three parts

PART I

In Richard's days, when lost his pastur'd plain,
The wand'ring Briton sought the wild wood's reign,
With great disdain beheld the feudal Hord,
Poor life-lett vassals of a Norman Lord;
And, what no brave man ever lost, possess'd   5
Himself,—for Freedom bound him to her Breast.
   Lov'st Thou that Freedom? By her holy shrine,
If yet one drop of British Blood be thine,
See, I conjure Thee, in the desart shade,
His Bow unstrung, his little household laid,   10
Some brave Forefather; while his Fields they share,
By Saxon, Dane, or Norman banish'd there!
And think He tells Thee, as his Soul withdraws,
As his Heart swells against a Tyrant's Laws,
The War with Fate though fruitless to maintain,   15
To guard that Liberty he lov'd in vain.
   Were thoughts like these the Dream of ancient Time?
Peculiar only to some Age, or Clime?
And does not Nature thoughts like these impart,
Breathe in the Soul, and write upon the Heart?   20
   Ask on their Mountains yon deserted Band,
That point to Paoli with no plausive Hand;

Despising still, their freeborn Souls unbroke,
Alike the *Gallic* and *Ligurian* Yoke!

Yet while the Patriot's gen'rous rage we share,   25
Still *civil Safety* calls us back to Care;—
To Britain lost in either Henry's day,
Her Woods, her Mountains one wild Scene of Prey!
Fair Peace from all her bounteous Vallies fled,
And Law beneath the barbed Arrow bled.   30

In happier Days, with more auspicious Fate,
The far-fam'd Edward heal'd his wounded State;
Dread of his Foes, but to his Subjects dear,
These learn'd to love, as those are taught to fear,
Their laurell'd Prince with British Pride obey,   35
His Glory shone their Discontent away,

With Care the tender Flow'r of Love to save,
And plant the Olive on *Disorder's* Grave,
For civil Storms fresh Barriers to provide,
He caught the fav'ring Calm and falling Tide.   40

The social Laws from Insult to protect,
To cherish Peace, to cultivate Respect;
The rich from wanton Cruelty restrain,
To smooth the Bed of Penury and Pain;
The hapless Vagrant to his Rest restore   45
The maze of Fraud, the Haunts of Theft explore;
The thoughtless Maiden, when subdu'd by Art,
To aid, and bring her Rover to her Heart;
Wild Riot's Voice with Dignity to quell,
Forbid unpeaceful Passions to rebel,   50
Wrest from Revenge the meditated Harm,
For this fair Justice rais'd her sacred Arm;
For this the rural Magistrate, of Yore,
Thy Honours, Edward, to his Mansion bore.

Oft, where old Air in conscious Glory fails,   55
On silver Waves that flow through smiling Vales;
In Harewood's Groves, where long my Youth was laid,

Unseen beneath their antient World of Shade;
With many a Group of antique Columns crown'd,
In Gothic Guise such Mansions have I found.   60
  Nor lightly deem, ye Apes of modern Race,
Ye Cits that sore bedizen Nature's Face,
Of the more manly Structures here ye view;
They rose for Greatness that ye never knew!
Ye reptile Cits, that oft have mov'd my Spleen   65
With Venus, and the Graces on your Green!
Let Plutus, growling o'er his ill-got Wealth,
Let Mercury, the thriving God of Stealth,
The Shopman, Janus, with his double Looks,
Rise on your Mounts, and perch upon your Books!   70
But spare my Venus, spare each Sister Grace,
Ye Cits, that sore bedizen Nature's Face!
  Ye royal Architects, whose antic Taste,
Would lay the Realms of Sense and Nature waste;
Forgot, whenever from her Steps ye stray,   75
That Folly only points each other way;
Here, tho' your Eye no *courtly* Creature sees,
Snakes on the ground, or *Monkies* in the Trees;
Yet let not too severe a Censure fall
On the plain Precincts of the antient Hall.   80
  For tho' no Sight your childish Fancy meets,
Of Thibet's Dogs, or China's Perroquets;
Tho' Apes, Asps, Lizards, Things without a Tail,
And all the Tribes of foreign Monsters fail;
Here shall ye sigh to see, with Rust o'ergrown,   85
The Iron Griffin and the Sphynx of Stone;
And mourn, neglected in their waste abodes,
Fire-breathing Drakes, and water-spouting Gods.
  Long have these mighty Monsters known Disgrace,
Yet still some Trophies hold their ancient place;   90
Where, round the Hall, the Oaks high surbase rears
The Field-day Triumphs of two hundred years.

73

Th'enormous Antlers here recall the day
That saw the Forest-Monarch *forc'd away*;
Who, many a Flood, and many a Mountain past,   95
Nor finding those, nor deeming these the last,
O'er Floods, o'er Mountains yet prepar'd to fly,
Long ere the Death-drop fill'd his failing Eye!

Here, fam'd for Cunning, and in Crimes grown old,
Hangs his grey Brush, the Felon of the Fold.   100
Oft as the Rent Feast swells the Midnight Cheer,
The Maudlin Farmer kens him o'er his Beer,
And tells his old, traditionary Tale,
Tho' known to ev'ry Tenant of the Vale.

Here, where, of old, the festal Ox has fed,   105
Mark'd with his weight, the mighty horns are spread:
Some Ox, O Marshall, for a Board like thine,
Where the vast Master with the vast Sirloin
Vied in round Magnitude—Respect I bear
To Thee, tho' oft the Ruin of the Chair.   110

These, and such antique Tokens, that record
The manly Spirit and the bounteous Board,
Me more delight than all the Gew-gaw Train,
The Whims and Zigzags of a modern Brain,
More than all Asia's Marmosets to view   115
Grin, frisk, and water in the Walks of Kew.

Thro' these fair Vallies, Stranger, hast Thou stray'd,
By any Chance, to visit Harewood's Shade,
And seen with honest, antiquated Air,
In the plain Hall the Magistratial Chair?   120
There Herbert sate—The Love of human kind,
Pure Light of Truth, and Temperance of Mind,
In the free Eye the featur'd Soul display'd,
Honour's strong Beam, and Mercy's melting Shade:
Justice, that in the rigid Paths of Law,   125
Would still some Drops from Pity's Fountain draw,
Bend o'er her Urn with many a gen'rous Fear,

Ere his firm Seal should force one Orphan's Tear;
Fair Equity, and Reason scorning Art,
And all the sober Virtues of the Heart,—   130
These sate with Herbert, these shall best avail,
Where Statutes order; or where Statutes fail.
  Be this, ye rural Magistrates, your Plan :
Firm be your Justice, but be Friends to Man.
  He whom the mighty Master of this Ball   135
We fondly deem, or farcically call,
To own the Patriach's Truth however loth,
Holds but a Mansion *crush'd before the Moth*.
  Frail in his Genius, in his Heart, too, frail,
Born but to err, and erring to bewail,   140
Shalt Thou his Faults with Eye severe explore,
And give to Life one human Weakness more?
  Still mark if Vice or Nature prompts the Deed;
Still mark the strong Temptation and the Need:
On pressing Want, on Famine's powerful call,   145
At least more lenient let thy Justice fall.
  For Him, who, lost to ev'ry Hope of Life,
Has long with Fortune held unequal strife,
Known to no human Love, no human Care,
The friendless, homeless Object of Despair;   150
For the poor Vagrant, feel, while He complains,
Nor from sad Freedom send to sadder Chains.
Alike, if Folly or Misfortune brought
Those last of Woes his evil Days have wrought;
Believe with social Mercy and with Me,   155
Folly's Misfortune in the first Degree.
  Perhaps on some inhospitable Shore
The houseless Wretch a widow'd Parent bore;
Who, then, no more by golden Prospects led,
Of the poor Indian begg'd a Leafy bed.   160
Cold on Canadian Hills, or Minden's Plain,
Perhaps that Parent mourned her Soldier slain;

Bent o'er her Babe, her Eye dissolv'd in Dew,
The big Drops mingling with the Milk He drew,
Gave the lad Presage of his future Years,   165
The Child of Misery, baptiz'd in Tears!

O Edward, here thy fairest Laurels fade!
And thy long Glories darken into Shade!

While yet the Palms thy hardy Veterans won,
The Deeds of Valour that for thee were done,   170
While yet the Wreaths for which they bravely bled,
Fir'd thy high Soul, and flourish'd on thy Head,
Those Veterans to their native Shores return'd,
Like Exiles wander'd, and like Exiles mourn'd;
Or, left *at large* no longer to bewail,   175
Were vagrants deem'd, and destined to a jail!

Were there no Royal, yet uncultur'd Lands,
No Wastes that wanted such subduing Hands?
Were Cressy's Heroes such abandon'd Things?
O Fate of War! and Gratitude of Kings!   180

The Gypsy-Race my Pity rarely move;
Yet their strong thirst of Liberty I love.
Not Wilkes, our Freedom's holy Martyr, more;
Nor his firm *Phalanx* of the common Shore.

For this in Norwood's patrimonial Groves   185
The tawny Father with his Offspring roves;
When Summer Suns lead slow the sultry Day,
In mossy Caves where welling Waters play,
Fann'd by each Gale that cools the fervid Sky,
With this in ragged Luxury they lie.   190
Oft at the Sun the dusky Elfins strain
The sable Eye, then, snugging, sleep again:
Oft, as the Dews of cooler Evening fall,
For their prophetic Mother's Mantle call.

Far other Cares that wand'ring Mother wait,   195
The Mouth, and oft the Minister, of Fate!
From her to hear, in Ev'ning's friendly shade,

Of future Fortune, flies the Village-Maid,
Draws her long-hoarded Copper from its hold;
And rusty Halfpence purchase hopes of Gold.   200
  But ah! ye Maids, beware the Gypsy's Lures!
She opens not the Womb of Time, but yours.
Oft has her Hands the hapless MARIAN wrung,
MARIAN, whom Gay in sweetest Strains has sung!
The Parson's Maid—sore Cause had she to rue   205
The Gypsy's Tongue; the Parson's Daughter too.
Long had that anxious Daughter sigh'd to know
What Vellum's sprucy Clerk, the Valley's Beau,
Meant by those Glances which at Church he stole,
Her Father nodding to the Psalm's slow Drawl;   210
Long had she sigh'd, at length a Prophet came,
By many a sure Prediction known to Fame,
To MARIAN known, and all she told, for true:
She knew the future, for the past she knew.
  Where, in the darkling Shed, the Moon's dim Rays 215
Beam'd on the Ruins of a One-Horse Chaise,
Villaria sat, while faithful MARIAN brought
The wayward Prophet of the Woe she sought.
Twice did her Hands, the Income of the Week,
On either side, the crooked Sixpence seek;   220
Twice were those Hands withdrawn from either side,
To stop the titt'ring Laugh, the Blush to hide.
The wayward Prophet made no long Delay,
No Novice she in Fortune's devious way!
'Ere yet, she cried, ten rolling months are o'er,   225
'Must ye be Mothers; Maids, at least, no more.
'With you shall soon, O Lady fair, prevail
'A gentle Youth, the Flower of this fair Vale.
'To MARIAN, once of Colin Clout the Scorn,
'Shall Bumkin come, and Bumkinets be born.'   230
  Smote to the Heart, the Maidens marvell'd sore,
That Ten short Months had such Events in store;

But holding firm what Village-Maids believe,
That Strife with Fate is milking in a Sieve;
To prove their Prophet true, though to their Cost,   235
They justly thought no Time was to be lost.
   These Foes to Youth, that seek, with dang'rous Art,
To aid the native Weakness of the Heart;
These Miscreants from thy harmless Village drive,
As Wasps felonious from the lab'ring Hive.   240

The Country Justice

To Robert Wilson Cracroft, Esq.

Born with a gentle Heart, and born to please
With native Goodness, of no Fortune vain,
The social Aspect of inviting Ease,
The kind Opinion, and the Sense humane;

To Thee, my CRACROFT, whom, in early Youth,
With lenient Hand, and anxious Love I led
Thro' Paths where Science points to manly Truth,
And Glory gilds the Mansions of the Dead:

To Thee this Offering of maturer Thought,
That, since wild FANCY flung the Lyre aside,
With heedful Hand the MORAL MUSE hath wrought,
That Muse devotes, and bears with honest Pride.

Yet not that Period of the human Year,
When FANCY reign'd, shall we with Pain review,
All NATURE's Seasons different Aspects wear,
And now her Flowers, and now her Fruits are due.

Not that in Youth we rang'd the smiling Meads,
On Essex' Shores the trembling Angle play'd,
Urging at Noon the slow Boat in the Reeds,
That wav'd their green Uncertainty of Shade:

Nor yet the Days consum'd in HACKTHORN's Vale,
That lonely on the Heath's wild Bosom lies,
Should we with stern Severity bewail,
And all the *lighter* Hours of Life despise.

For Nature's Seasons different Aspects wear,
And now her Flowers, and now her Fruits are due;
Awhile she freed us from the Scourge of CARE,
But told us *then*—for social Ends we grew.

To find some Virtue trac'd on Life's short Page,
Some Mark of Service paid to human Kind,
Alone can chear the wint'ry Paths of Age,
Alone support the far-reflecting Mind.

Oh! often thought—when SMITH's discerning Care
To further Days prolong'd this failing Frame!
To die was little—But what Heart could bear
To die, and leave an undistinguish'd Name?

Blagdon House,
  22 Feb. 1775.

PART II

Yet, while thy Rod restrains the needy Crew,
Remember that Thou art their Monarch too.
KING OF THE BEGGARS!—Lov'st Thou not the Name?
O, great from GANGES to the golden Tame!
Far-ruling Sovereign of this begging Ball,   5
Low at thy Footstool other Thrones shall fall.
His Alms to Thee the whisker'd Moor convey,
And PRUSSIA's sturdy Beggar own thy Sway;
Courts, Senates—all to BAAL that bend the Knee,
King of the Beggars, these are Fiefs to Thee!   10
    But still, forgot the Grandeur of thy Reign,
Descend to Duties meaner Crowns disdain;
That worst Excrescency of Power forego,
That *Pride* of Kings, Humanity's first Foe.
    Let Age no longer toil with feeble Strife,   15
Worn by long Service in the War of Life;
Nor leave the Head, that Time hath whiten'd, bare
To the rude Insults of the searching Air;
Nor bid the Knee, by Labour harden'd, bend,
O Thou, the poor Man's Hope, the poor Man's Friend!   20
    If, when from Heav'n severer Seasons fall,
Fled from the frozen Roof, and mouldering Wall,
Each Face the Picture of a Winter-Day,
More strong than *Teniers*' Pencil could pourtray;—
If then to Thee resort the shivering Train,   25
Of cruel Days, and cruel Man complain,
Say to thy Heart (remembering Him who said)
These People come from far, and have no Bread.
    Nor leave thy venal Clerk empower'd to hear;
The Voice of Want is sacred to *thy* Ear.   30
He, where no Fees his sordid Pen invite,

Sports with their Tears, too indolent to write;
Like the fed Monkey in the Fable, vain
To hear more helpless Animals complain.
  But chief thy Notice shall One Monster claim,   35
A Monster furnished with a human Frame,
The Parish-Officer!—though VERSE disdain
Terms that deform the Splendor of the Strain;
It stoops to bid Thee bend the Brow severe
On the sly, pilfering, cruel Overseer;   40
The shuffling Farmer, faithful to no Trust,
Ruthless as Rocks, insatiate as the Dust!
  When the poor Hind, with Length of Years decay'd,
Leans feebly on his once subduing Spade,
Forgot the Service of his abler Days,   45
His profitable Toil, and honest Praise,
Shall this low Wretch abridge his scanty Bread,
This Slave, whose Board his former Labours spread?
  When Harvest's burning Suns and sickening Air
From Labour's unbrac'd Hand the grasp'd Hook tear, 50
Where shall the helpless Family be fed,
That vainly languish for a Father's Bread?
See the pale Mother, sunk with Grief and Care,
To the proud Farmer fearfully repair;
Soon to be sent with Insolence away,   55
Referr'd to Vestries, and a distant Day!
Referr'd—to perish!—Is my verse severe?
Unfriendly to the human Character?
Ah! to this Sigh of sad Experience trust:
The Truth is rigid, but the Tale is just.   60
  If in thy Courts this Caitiff Wretch appear,
Think not, that Patience were a Virtue here.
His low-born Pride with honest Rage controul;
Smite his hard Heart, and shake his Reptile Soul.
  But, hapless! oft thro' Fear of future Woe,   65
And certain Vengeance of th' insulting Foe,

Oft, ere to Thee the Poor prefer their Pray'r,
The last Extremes of Penury they bear.
  Wouldst Thou then raise thy Patriot Office higher,
To something more than Magistrate aspire?   70
And, left each poorer, pettier Chace behind,
Step nobly forth, the Friend of Human Kind?
The Game I start courageously pursue!
Adieu to Fear! to Insolence adieu!
And first we'll range this Mountain's stormy Side,   75
Where the rude Winds the Shepherd's Roof deride,
As meet no more the wintry Blast to bear,
And all the wild Hostilities of Air.
—That Roof have I remember'd many a Year;
It once gave Refuge to a hunted Deer—   80
Here, in those Days, we found an aged Pair;—
But TIME untenants—Hah! what seest Thou there?
'Horror—by Heav'n, extended on a Bed
'Of naked Fearn, two human Creatures dead!
'Embracing as alive!—ah, no!—no Life!   85
'Cold, breathless!'
                    'Tis the Shepherd and his Wife.
I knew the Scene, and brought Thee to behold
What speaks more strongly than the story told.
They died thro' Want—
                    'By every Power I swear,
'If the Wretch treads the Earth, or breathes the Air,   90
'Thro' whose Default of Duty, or Design,
'These Victims fell, he dies.'
                    They fell by thine.
'Infernal!—Mine!—by—'
                    Swear on no Pretence:
A swearing Justice wants both Grace and Sense.
  When thy good Father held this wide Domain,   95
The Voice of Sorrow never mourn'd in vain.
Sooth'd by his Pity, by his Bounty fed,

The Sick found Medicine, and the Agèd Bread.
He left their Interest to no Parish-Care,
No Bailiff urg'd his little Empire there: 100
No Village-Tyrant starv'd them, or oppress'd;
He learn'd their Wants, and He those Wants redress'd.
   Ev'n these, unhappy! who, behold too late,
Smote thy young Heart with Horror at their Fate,
His Bounty found, and destin'd here to keep   105
A small Detachment of his Mountain-Sheep.
Still pleas'd to see them from the annual Fair
Th' unwritten History of their Profits bear;
More nobly pleas'd those Profits to restore,
And, if their Fortune fail'd them, make it more.   110
   When Nature gave her Precept to remove
His kindred Spirit to the Realms of Love,
Afar their Anguish from thy distant Ear,
No Arm to save, and no Protection near,
Led by the Lure of unaccounted Gold,   115
Thy Bailiff seiz'd their little Flock, and Sold.
   Their Want contending Parishes survey'd,
And this disown'd, and that refus'd to aid:
Awhile, who should *not* succour them, they tried,
And in that while the wretched Victims died.   120
   'I'll scalp that Bailiff—sacrifice.'
                       In vain
To rave at Mischief, if the Cause remain!
   O Days long lost to Man in each Degree!
The golden Days of Hospitality!
When liberal Fortunes vied with liberal Strife,   125
To fill the noblest Offices of Life;
When WEALTH was Virtue's Handmaid, and her Gate
Gave a free Refuge from the Wrongs of Fate;
The Poor at Hand their natural Patrons saw,
And Lawgivers were Supplements of Law!   130
   Lost are those Days, and FASHION's boundless Sway

Has borne the Guardian Magistrate away.
Save in AUGUSTA's Streets, or Gallia's Shore,
The Rural Patron is beheld no more.
No more the Poor his kind Protection share,   135
Unknown their Wants, and unreceiv'd their Prayer.

Yet has that Fashion, long so light and vain,
Reform'd at last, and led the moral Train?
Have her gay Vot'ries nobler worth to boast
For NATURE's Love, for NATURE's Virtue lost?   140
No—fled from these, the Sons of Fortune find
What poor Respect to Wealth remains behind.
The Mock Regard alone of menial Slaves,
The worship'd Calves of their outwitting Knaves!

Foregone the social, hospitable Days,   145
When wide Vales echoed with their Owner's Praise,
Of all that *ancient Consequence* bereft,
What has the *modern Man of Fashion left*?

Does He, perchance, to rural Scenes repair,
And 'waste his Sweetness' on the essenc'd Air?   150
Ah! gently lave the feeble Frame He brings,
Ye scouring Seas! and ye sulphureous Springs!

And thou, Brightelmstone, where no Cits annoy,
(All borne to MARGATE, in the Margate-Hoy)
Where, if the hasty Creditor advance,   155
Lies the light Skiff, and ever-bailing France,
Do Thou defend Him in the Dog-Day-Suns!
Secure in Winter from the Rage of Duns!

While the grim Catchpole, the grim Porter swear,
One that He is, and one, He is not there,   160
The tortur'd Us'rer, as he murmurs by,
Eyes the Venetian Blinds, and heaves a Sigh.

O, from each Title Folly ever took,
Blood! Maccorone! Cicisbeo! or Rook!
From each low Passion, from each low Resort,   165
The thieving Alley, nay, the righteous Court,

From BERTIE's, ALMACK's, ARTHUR's, and the Nest
Where JUDAH's Ferrets earth with CHARLES unblest;—
From these and all the Garbage of the great,
At Honour's, Freedom's, Virtue's Call—retreat!   170
    Has the fair Vale, where REST, conceal'd in Flowers,
Lies in Sweet Ambush for thy careless Hours,
The Breeze, that, balmy Fragrance to infuse,
Bathes its soft Wing in Aromatic Dews,
The Stream, to soothe thine Ear, to cool thy Breast,   175
That mildly murmurs from its crystal Rest;—
Have these less Charms to win, less Power to please,
Than Haunts of Rapine, Harbours of Disease?
    Will no kind Slumbers o'er thine Eyelids creep,
Save where the sullen Watchman growls at Sleep?   180
Does Morn no sweeter, purer Breath diffuse
Than streams thro' Alleys from the Lungs of JEWS?
And is thy Water, pent in putrid Wood,
BETHESDA-like, when troubled *only* good?
    Is it thy Passion LINLEY's Voice to hear,   185
And has no Mountain-Lark detain'd thine Ear?
Song marks alone the Tribes of Airy Wing;
For, trust Me, Man was never meant to sing:
And all his Mimic Organs e'er exprest,
Was but an imitative Howl at best.   190
    Is it on GARRICK's Attitude you doat?
See on the pointed Cliff your lordly Goat!
Like LEAR's, his Beard descends in graceful Snow,
And wild He looks upon the World below.
    Superior *here* the Scene in every Part!   195
Here reigns great Nature, and there little Art!
Here let thy Life assume a nobler Plan,
To Nature faithful, and the Friend of Man!
    Unnumber'd Objects ask thy honest Care,
Beside the Orphan's Tear, the Widow's Prayer.   200
Far as thy Power can save, thy Bounty bless,

Unnumber'd Evils call for thy Redress.
   Seest Thou afar yon solitary Thorn,
Whose agèd *Limbs* the Heath's wild Winds have torn?
While yet to cheer the homeward Shepherd's Eye,   205
A *few* seem straggling in the Evening Sky!
Not many Suns have hasten'd down the Day,
Or blushing Moons immers'd in Clouds their Way,
Since there a Scene, that Stain'd their sacred Light,
With Horror stopp'd a Felon in his Flight;   210
A Babe just born that Signs of Life exprest,
Lay naked o'er the Mother's lifeless Breast.
The pitying Robber, conscious that, pursued,
He had no Time to waste, yet stood and view'd;
To the next Cot the trembling Infant bore,   215
And gave a Part of what He stole before;
Nor known to Him the Wretches were, nor dear,
He felt as Man, and dropp'd a human Tear.
   Far other Treatment She who breathless lay,
Found from a viler Animal of Prey.   220
   Worn with long Toil on many a painful Road,
That Toil increas'd by Nature's growing Load,
When Evening brought the friendly Hour of Rest,
And all the Mother throng'd about her Breast,
The Ruffian Officer oppos'd her Stay,   225
And, cruel, bore her in her Pangs away,
So far beyond the Town's last Limits drove,
That to return were hopeless, had She strove.
Abandon'd there—with Famine, Pain, and Cold,
And Anguish, She expir'd—the rest I've told.   230
   'Now *let* Me swear—For, by my Soul's last Sigh,
'That Thief shall live, that Overseer shall die.'
   Too late!—His Life the generous Robber paid
Lost by that Pity which his Steps delay'd!
No Soul-discerning MANSFIELD sat to hear,   235
No HERTFORD bore his Prayer to Mercy's ear;

No liberal Justice first assign'd the Gaol,
Or urg'd, as CAMPLIN would have urg'd his Tale.
  The living Object of thy honest Rage,
Old in Parochial Crimes, and *steel'd* with Age,   240
The grave Church-warden!—unabash'd He bears
Weekly to Church his Book of wicked Prayers;
And pours, with all the Blasphemy of Praise,
His creeping Soul in Sternhold's creeping Lays!   244

The Country Justice

PART III

O no! Sir John—the Muse's gentle Art
Lives not to blemish, but to mend the Heart.
While Gay's brave Robber grieves us for his Fate,
We hold the Harpies of his Life in Hate.
Ingenious Youth, by NATURE's Voice addrest,   5
Finds not the harden'd, but the feeling Breast;
Can form no Wish the dire Effects to prove
Of lawless Valour, or of venal Love.
Approves the Fondness of the faithful Maid,
And mourns a generous Passion unrepaid.   10
   Yet would I praise the pious Zeal that saves
Imperial London from her World of Knaves;
Yet would I count it no inglorious Strife,
To scourge the Pests of Property and Life.
   Come then, long skill'd in Theft's illusive Ways,   15
Lord of the Clue that threds her mighty Maze!
Together let us beat all Giles's Fields,
Try what the Night-House, what the Round-House yields,
Hang when we must, be candid when we please,
But leave no Bawd, unlicens'd, at her Ease.   20
   Say first, of Thieves above, or Thieves below,
What can we order till their Haunts we know?
Far from St. James's let your Nimrods stray,
But stop and call at Stephen's in their Way.
That ancient Victualler, we've been told, of late,   25
Has kept bad Hours, encourag'd high Debate;
That Those without still pelting Those within,
Have stunn'd the peaceful Neighbours with their Din;

That if you close his private Walls invest,
'Tis odds, you meet with some unruly Guest—   30
Good Lord, Sir John, how would the People stare,
To see the present and the late Lord Mayor
Bow to the Majesty of Bow-Street Chair!
    Illustrious Chiefs; can I your Haunts pass by,
Nor give my long-lov'd Liberty a Sigh?   35
That heavenly Plant which long unblemish'd blew,
Dishonour'd only, only hurt by You!
Dishonour'd, when with harden'd Front you claim
To Deeds of Darkness her diviner Name!
For you grim LICENCE strove with Hydra Breath   40
To spread the Blasts of Pestilence and Death:
Here for poor Vice, for dark Ambition there
She scatter'd Poison through the social Air.
Yet here, in vain—Oh, had her Toil been vain
When with black Wing she swept the Western Main!   45
When with low Labour, and insidious Art,
She tore a Daughter from her Parent's Heart!
    Oh, Patriots, ever Patriots out of Place,
Fair Honour's Foil, and Liberty's Disgrace!
With Spleen I see your wild Illusions spread,   50
Through the long Region of a Land misled;
See Commerce sink, see Cultivation's Charms
Lost in the Rage of Anarchy and Arms!
    And Thou, O Ch-m, once a Nation's Pride,
Borne on the brightest Wave of Glory's Tide!   55
Hast Thou the Parent spurn'd, the erring Child
With Prospect vain to Ruin's Arms beguil'd?
Hast Thou the Plans of dire Defection prais'd
For the poor Pleasure of a Statue rais'd?
    Oh, Patriots, ever Patriots out of Place,   60
From CHARLES quite graceless, up to GRAFTON's Grace!
    Where Forty-five once mark'd the dirty Door,
And the chain'd Knife invites the paltry Whore;

Though far, methinks, the choicest Guests are fled,
And WILKES and HUMPHREY number'd with the Dead, 65
Wilkes, who in Death would Friendship's Vows fulfil,
True to his Cause, and dines with Humphrey still—
Where sculks each dark, where roams each desperate Wight,
Owls of the Day and Vultures of the Night,—
Shall We, O Knight, with cruel Pains explore, 70
Clear these low Walks, and think the Bus'ness o'er?
No—much, alas! for You, for Me remains,
Where Justice sleeps, and Depredation reigns.
    Wrapt in kind Darkness, You no Spleen betray,
When the gilt Nabob lacqueys all the Way: 75
Harmless to You his Towers, his Forests rise,
That swell with Anguish my indignant Eyes;
While in those Towers raz'd Villages I see,
And Tears of Orphans watering every Tree.
Are these mock Ruins that invade my View? 80
These are the Entrails of the poor Gentoo.
That Column's trophied Base his Bones supply;
That Lake the Tears that swell'd his sable Eye!
Let here, O Knight, their Steps terrific steer
Thy *hue and cry*, and loose thy Bloodhounds here. 85
    Oh, Mercy, thron'd on His eternal Breast,
Who breath'd the savage Waters into Rest;
By each soft Pleasure that my Bosom smote,
When first Creation started from His Thought;
By each warm Tear that melted o'er Thine Eye, 90
When on his Works was written, These must die!
If secret Slaughter yet, nor cruel War
Have from these mortal Regions forc'd Thee far,
Still to our Follies, to our Frailties blind,
Oh, stretch thy healing Wings o'er Human Kind! 95
—For *them* I ask not, hostile to Thy Sway,
Who calmly on a Brother's Vitals prey:
For *them* I plead not, who, in Blood embrued,

Have every softer Sentiment subdued.

    Yet, gentle Power, thy Absence I bewail,   100
When seen the dark, dark Regions of a Gaol;
When found alike in Chains and Night enclos'd,
The Thief detected, and the Thief suppos'd!
Sure, the fair Light and the salubrious Air
Each yet-suspected Prisoner might share.   105
—To lie, to languish in some dreary Cell,
Some loathèd Hold, where Guilt and Horror dwell,
Ere yet the Truth of seeming Facts be tried,
Ere yet their Country's sacred Voice decide,
Britain, behold thy Citizens expos'd,   110
And blush to think the Gothic Age unclos'd!

    Oh, more than Goths, who yet decline to raze
That Pest of James's puritanic Days,
The savage Law that barb'rously ordains
For female Virtue lost a Felon's Pains!—   115
Dooms the poor Maiden, as her Fate severe,
To toil in chains a long-enduring Year.

    Th' unnatural Monarch, to the Sex unkind,
An Owl obscene, in Learning's Sunshine blind!
Councils of Pathics, Cabinets of Tools,   120
Benches of Knaves, and Parliaments of Fools!
Fanatic Fools, that, in those twilight Times,
With wild Religion cloak'd the worst of Crimes!
Hope we from such a Crew, in such a Reign,
For equal Laws, or Policy humane?   125

    Here, then, O JUSTICE, thy own Power forbear;
The sole Protector of th' unpitied Fair.
Though long entreat the ruthless Overseer;
Though the loud Vestry teaze thy tortur'd Ear;
Though all to Acts, to Precedents appeal,   130
Mute be thy Pen, and vacant rest thy Seal.

    Yet shalt thou know, nor is the Difference nice,
The casual Fall, from Impudence of Vice.

Abandon'd Guilt by active Laws restrain,
But pause . . . if Virtue's slightest Spark remain.   135
Left to the shameless Lash, the hard'ning Gaol,
The fairest Thoughts of Modesty would fail.

The down-cast Eye, the Tear that flows amain,
As if to ask her Innocence again;
The plaintive Babe, that slumbering seem'd to lie   140
On her soft Breast, and wakes at the heav'd Sigh;
The Cheek that wears the beauteous Robe of Shame;
How loth they leave a gentle Breast to blame!

Here, then, O JUSTICE thy own Power forbear;—
The sole Protector of th' unpitied Fair!   145

WILLIAM COWPER

Yardley-Oak

Survivor sole, and hardly such, of all,
That once liv'd here, thy brethren, at my birth,
Since which I number three-score winters past,
A shattered vet'ran, hollow-trunk'd perhaps,
As now, and with excoriate forks deform,   5
Relicts of ages, could a mind, imbu'd
With truth from Heav'n, created thing adore,
I might with rev'rence kneel, and worship thee!

It seems idolatry with some excuse,
When our fore-father Druids in their oaks   10
Imagin'd sanctity. The conscience, yet
Unpurify'd by an authentic act
Of amnesty, the meed of blood divine,
Lov'd not the light, but, gloomy, into gloom
Of thickest shades, like Adam after taste   15
Of fruit proscrib'd, as to a refuge, fled.

Thou wast a bauble once, a cup and ball,
Which babes might play with; and the thievish jay,
Seeking her food, with ease might have purloin'd
The auburn nut, that held thee, swallow'ing down   20
Thy yet close-folded latitude of boughs
And all thine embryo vastness at a gulp.
But Fate thy growth decreed; autumnal rains
Beneath thy parent tree mellow'd the soil

93

Design'd thy cradle; and a skipping deer,   25
With pointed hoof dibbling the glebe, prepar'd
The soft receptacle, in which, secure,
Thy rudiments should sleep the winter through.

So Fancy dreams. Disprove it, if ye can,
Ye reas'ners broad awake, whose busy search   30
Of argument, employ'd too oft amiss,
Sifts half the pleasures of short life away!

Thou fell'st mature, and, in the loamy clod
Swelling with vegetative force instinct,
Didst burst thine egg, as theirs the fabled Twins,   35
Now stars. Two lobes, protruding, pair'd exact;
A leaf succeeded, and another leaf,
And, all the elements thy puny growth
Fost'ring propitious, thou becam'st a twig.
Who liv'd, when thou wast such? Oh, couldst thou speak,   40
As in Dodona once thy kindred trees
Oracular, I would not curious ask
The future, best unknown, but at thy mouth
Inquisitive, the less ambiguous past!

By thee I might correct, erroneous oft,   45
The clock of history, facts and events
Timing more punctual, unrecorded facts
Recov'ring, and mistated setting right—
Desp'rate attempt, till trees shall speak again!

Time made thee what thou wast, king of the woods;   50
And Time hath made thee what thou art—a cave
For owls to roost in! Once thy spreading boughs
O'erhung the champaign; and the numerous flocks,
That graz'd it, stood beneath that ample cope
Uncrouded, yet safe-shelter'd from the storm.   55

No flock frequents thee now. Thou hast out-liv'd
Thy popularity, and art become
(Unless verse rescue thee awhile) a thing
Forgotten, as the foliage of thy youth!

    While thus through all the stages thou hast push'd   60
Of treeship—first a seedling, hid in grass;
Then twig; then sapling; and, as cent'ry roll'd
Slow after century, a giant-bulk
Of girth enormous, with moss-cushion'd root
Upheav'd above the soil, and sides imboss'd   65
With promi'nent wens globose—till at the last,
The rottenness, which time is charg'd to'inflict
On other mighty ones, found also thee.

    What exhibitions various hath the world
Witness'd of mutability in all,   70
That we account most durable below!
Change is the diet, on which all subsist,
Created changeable, and change at last
Destroys them. Skies uncertain, now the heat
Transmitting cloudless, and the solar beam   75
Now quenching in a boundless sea of clouds,
Calm, and alternate storm, moisture, and drought,
Invigorate by turns the springs of life
In all that live, plant, animal, and man,
And in conclusion mar them. Nature's threads,   80
Fine, passing thought, e'en in her coarsest works,
Delight in agitation, yet sustain
The force, that agitates, not unimpair'd,
But, worn by frequent impulse, to the cause
Of their best tone their dissolution owe.   85
    Thought cannot spend itself, comparing still
The great and little of thy lot, thy growth
From almost nullity into a state

Of matchless grandeur, and declension thence,
Slow, into such magnificent decay.   90
Time was, when, settling on thy leaf, a fly
Could shake thee to the root—and time has been
When tempests could not. At thy firmest age
Thou hadst within thy bole solid contents,
That might have ribb'd the sides and plank'd the deck   95
Of some flagg'd admiral, and tortuous arms,
The ship-wright's darling treasure, didst present
To the four quarter'd winds, robust and bold,
Warp'd into tough knee-timber, many a load!
But the axe spar'd thee. In those thriftier days   100
Oaks fell not, hewn by thousands, to supply
The bottomless demands of contest, wag'd
For senatorial honours. Thus to Time
The task was left to whittle thee away
With his sly scythe, whose ever-nibbling edge,   105
Noiseless, an atom, and an atom more,
Disjoining from the rest, has, unobserv'd,
Achiev'd a labour, which had far and wide,
By man perform'd, made all the forest ring.
  Embowell'd now, and of thy ancient self   110
Possessing nought, but the scoop'd rind, that seems
An huge throat, calling to the clouds for drink,
Which it would give in rivu'lets to thy root;
Thou temptest none, but rather much forbidd'st
The feller's toil, which thou could'st ill requite.   115
  Yet is thy root sincere, sound as the rock,
A quarry of stout spurs, and knotted fangs,
Which, crook'd into a thousand whimsies, clasp
The stubborn soil, and hold thee still erect.

  So stands a kingdom, whose foundation yet   120
Fails not, in virtue and in wisdom laid,
Tho' all the superstructure, by the tooth

Pulveriz'd of venality, a shell
Stands now and semblance only of itself!

Thine arms have left thee. Winds have torn them off   125
Long since, and rovers of the forest wild,
With bow and shaft, have burnt them. Some have left
A splinter'd stump, bleach'd to a snowy white;
And some, memorial none where once they grew.
Yet still life lingers in thee, and puts forth   130
Proof not contemptible of what she can,
Even where death predominates. The spring
Finds thee not less alive to her sweet force,
Than yonder upstarts of the neighb'ring wood,
So much thy juniors, who their birth receiv'd   135
Half a millennium since the date of thine.

But since, although well qualify'd by age
To teach, no spirit dwells in thee, nor voice
May be expected from thee, seated here
On thy distorted root, with hearers none,   140
Or prompter, save the scene, I will perform
Myself the oracle, and will discourse
In my own ear such matter as I may.

One man alone, the father of us all,
Drew not his life from woman; never gaz'd,   145
With mute unconsciousness of what he saw,
On all around him; learn'd not by degrees,
Nor ow'd articulation to his ear;
But, moulded by his Maker into man
At once, upstood intelligent, survey'd   150
All creatures, with precision understood
Their purport, uses, properties, assign'd
To each his name significant, and, fill'd
With love and wisdom, render'd back to Heav'n

In praise harmonious the first air he drew.   155
He was excus'd the penalties of dull
Minority. No tutor charg'd his hand
With the thought-tracing quill, or task'd his mind
With problems. History, not wanted yet,
Lean'd on her elbow, watching Time, whose course,   160
Eventful, should supply her with a theme;—

WILLIAM WORDSWORTH

The Old Cumberland Beggar

I saw an agèd Beggar in my walk;
And he was seated, by the highway side,
On a low structure of rude masonry
Built at the foot of a huge hill, that they
Who lead their horses down the steep rough road   5
May thence remount at ease. The agèd Man
Had placed his staff across the broad smooth stone
That overlays the pile; and, from a bag
All white with flour, the dole of village dames,
He drew his scraps and fragments, one by one;   10
And scanned them with a fixed and serious look
Of idle computation. In the sun,
Upon the second step of that small pile,
Surrounded by those wild unpeopled hills,
He sat, and ate his food in solitude: 15
And ever, scattered from his palsied hand,
That, still attempting to prevent the waste,
Was baffled still, the crumbs in little showers
Fell on the ground; and the small mountain birds,
Not venturing yet to peck their destined meal,   20
Approached within the length of half his staff.
   Him from my childhood have I known; and then
He was so old, he seems not older now;
He travels on, a solitary Man,
So helpless in appearance, that for him   25
The sauntering Horseman throws not with a slack

And careless hand his alms upon the ground,
But stops,—that he may safely lodge the coin
Within the old Man's hat; nor quits him so,
But still, when he has given his horse the rein,   30
Watches the agèd Beggar with a look
Sidelong, and half-reverted. She who tends
The toll-gate, when in summer at her door
She turns her wheel, if on the road she sees
The agèd beggar coming, quits her work,   35
And lifts the latch for him that he may pass.
The post-boy, when his rattling wheels o'ertake
The agèd Beggar in the woody lane,
Shouts to him from behind; and if, thus warned,
The old man does not change his course, the boy   40
Turns with less noisy wheels to the road-side
And passes gently by, without a curse
Upon his lips, or anger at his heart.

He travels on, a solitary Man;
His age has no companion. On the ground   45
His eyes are turned, and, as he moves along
They move along the ground; and, evermore,
Instead of common and habitual sight
Of fields with rural works, of hill and dale,
And the blue sky, one little span of earth   50
Is all his prospect. Thus, from day to day,
Bow-bent, his eyes for ever on the ground,
He plies his weary journey; seeing still,
And seldom knowing that he sees, some straw,
Some scattered leaf, or marks which, in one track,   55
The nails of cart or chariot-wheel have left
Impressed on the white road,—in the same line,
At distance still the same. Poor Traveller!
His staff trails with him; scarcely do his feet
Disturb the summer dust; he is so still   60
In look and motion, that the cottage curs,

Ere he has passed the door, will turn away,
Weary of barking at him. Boys and girls,
The vacant and the busy, maids and youths,
And urchins newly breeched—all pass him by: 65
Him even the slow-paced waggon leaves behind.
   But deem not this Man useless.—Statesmen! ye
Who are so restless in your wisdom, ye
Who have a broom still ready in your hands
To rid the world of nuisances; ye proud,   70
Heart-swoln, while in your pride ye contemplate
Your talents, power, or wisdom, deem him not
A burthen of the earth! 'Tis Nature's law
That none, the meanest of created things,
Or forms created the most vile and brute,   75
The dullest or most noxious, should exist
Divorced from good—a spirit and pulse of good,
A life and soul, to every mode of being
Inseparably linked. Then be assured
That least of all can aught—that ever owned   80
The heaven-regarding eye and front sublime
Which man is born to—sink, howe'er depressed,
So low as to be scorned without a sin;
Without offence to God cast out of view;
Like the dry remnant of a garden-flower   85
Whose seeds are shed, or as an implement
Worn out and worthless. While from door to door,
This old Man creeps, the villagers in him
Behold a record which together binds
Past deeds and offices of charity,   90
Else unremembered, and so keeps alive
The kindly mood in hearts which lapse of years,
And that half-wisdom half-experience gives,
Make slow to feel, and by sure steps resign
To selfishness and cold oblivious cares.   95
Among the farms and solitary huts,

Hamlets and thinly scattered villages,
Where'er the agèd Beggar takes his rounds,
The mild necessity of use compels
To acts of love; and habit does the work   100
Of reason; yet prepares that after-joy
Which reason cherishes. And thus the soul,
By that sweet taste of pleasure unpursued,
Doth find herself insensibly disposed
To virtue and true goodness.

                    Some there are,   105
By their good works exalted, lofty minds
And meditative, authors of delight
And happiness, which to the end of time
Will live, and spread, and kindle: even such minds
In childhood, from this solitary Being,   110
Or from like wanderer, haply have received
(A thing more precious far than all that books
Or the solicitudes of love can do!)
That first mild touch of sympathy and thought,
In which they found their kindred with a world   115
Where want and sorrow were. The easy man
Who sits at his own door—and, like the pear
That overhangs his head from the green wall,
Feeds in the sunshine; the robust and young,
The prosperous and unthinking, they who live   120
Sheltered, and flourish in a little grove
Of their own kindred;—all behold in him
A silent monitor, which on their minds
Must needs impress a transitory thought
Of self-congratulation, to the heart   125
Of each recalling his peculiar boons
His charters and exemptions; and, perchance,
Though he to no one give the fortitude
And circumspection needful to preserve
His present blessings, and to husband up   130

The respite of the season, he, at least,
And 'tis no vulgar service, makes them felt.
  Yet further.—Many, I believe, there are
Who live a life of virtuous decency,
Men who can hear the Decalogue and feel   135
No self-reproach; who of the moral law
Established in the land where they abide
Are strict observers; and not negligent
In acts of love to those with whom they dwell,
Their kindred, and the children of their blood.   140
Praise be to such, and to their slumbers peace!
—But of the poor man ask, the abject poor;
Go, and demand of him, if there be here
In this cold abstinence from evil deeds,
And these inevitable charities,   145
Wherewith to satisfy the human soul?
No—man is dear to man; the poorest poor
Long for some moments in a weary life
When they can know and feel that they have been,
Themselves, the fathers and the dealers-out   150
Of some small blessings; have been kind to such
As needed kindness, for this single cause,
That we have all of us one human heart.
—Such pleasure is to one kind Being known,
My neighbour, when with punctual care, each week 155
Duly as Friday comes, though pressed herself
By her own wants, she from her store of meal
Takes one unsparing handful for the scrip
Of this old Mendicant, and, from her door
Returning with exhilarated heart,   160
Sits by her fire, and builds her hope in heaven.
  Then let him pass, a blessing on his head!
And while in that vast solitude to which
The tide of things has borne him, he appears
To breathe and live but for himself alone,   165

Unblamed, uninjured, let him bear about
The good which the benignant law of Heaven
Has hung around him: and, while life is his,
Still let him prompt the unlettered villagers
To tender offices and pensive thoughts.   170
—Then let him pass, a blessing on his head!
And, long as he can wander, let him breathe
The freshness of the valleys; let his blood
Struggle with frosty air and winter snows;
And let the chartered wind that sweeps the heath   175
Beat his grey locks against his withered face.
Reverence the hope whose vital anxiousness
Gives the last human interest to his heart.
May never HOUSE, misnamed of INDUSTRY,
Make him a captive!—for that pent-up din,   180
Those life-consuming sounds that clog the air,
Be his the natural silence of old age!
Let him be free of mountain solitudes;
And have around him, whether heard or not,
The pleasant melody of woodland birds.   185
Few are his pleasures: if his eyes have now
Been doomed so long to settle upon earth
That not without some effort they behold
The countenance of the horizontal sun,
Rising or setting, let the light at least   190
Find a free entrance to their languid orbs.
And let him, *where* and *when* he will, sit down
Beneath the trees, or on a grassy bank
Of highway side, and with the little birds
Share his chance-gathered meal; and, finally,   195
As in the eye of Nature he has lived,
So in the eye of Nature let him die!

NOTES

I. THE SCHOOL-MISTRESS   published 1737-1748

The School-Mistress, when it first appeared in 1737 in Shenstone's *Poems upon Various Occasions,* consisted of only 12 stanzas; a new version in 1742 ran to 28 stanzas; and the final version, in the 2nd edition of Dodsley's *Collection of Poems by Several Hands* (1748), was 35 stanzas long. This last is the version here given. Like most of the Spenserian imitations, it was first conceived as a burlesque, but the author became more serious about it, as it developed. See Virginia L. Prettyman in *The Age of Johnson. Studies presented to Chauncey Brewster Tinker.*

Johnson in his *Life of Shenstone* discriminated very justly the pleasure to be obtained from the imitation as from no other poetic form: 'The adoption of a particular style, in light and short compositions, contributes much to the increase of pleasure: we are entertained at once with two imitations, of nature in the sentiments, of the original author in the style, and between them the mind is kept in perpetual employment.' Johnson also records that the old schoolmistress whom Shenstone commemorates was the dame of the school where the poet learned to read.

WILLIAM SHENSTONE, born in 1714, was brought up by his grandmother, and studied at Pembroke College, Oxford. His principal interest in life was the beautifying of his small country estate, the Leasowes, which in other respects he did not manage to any profit. Johnson says, 'He spent his estate in adorning it, and his death was probably hastened by his anxieties.' He died unmarried in 1763.

2. *st.*3.   Note the felicity of *tingled.*

3. *st.*6.   *tway:* 'two' (archaism). cf. Spenser, *Shepheardes Calender,* 'May': 'We tway bene men of elder witt.'
   The rhyme on 'join'd' and 'unkind' was a true rhyme according to the early eighteenth-century pronunciation of 'join'.

   *st.*7.   'LIBS, NOTUS, AUSTER': classical names for the winds. 'Notus' is the Greek word, 'Auster' the Latin, for the same wind. 'Childish' as portrayed, cherubic, by old cartographers.

4. *st.*8.   Note the reference to cottage industry.

5. *st.*11, 12, 13. Compare with this catalogue of herbs, Spenser's of trees in *The Faerie Queene*, Canto 1, sts. 8 and 9; but even more strikingly the catalogue of herbs in Spenser's *Muiopotmos*, sts. 24 and 25.

*st.*13. *wassel:* wassail, i.e. 'festal'.

6. *st.*14. 'STERNHOLD': Thomas Sternhold, author with John Hopkins of the metrical psalms, died in 1549.

*st.*15. *lawny:* with lawn-sleeves; a reference to the martyred bishops like Cranmer. In this stanza, one of those added in 1745, Shenstone expresses the fear of popery generally re-awakened by the Jacobite rising of that year.

7. *st.*19. *the bard by* MULLA's *stream:* Spenser. 'Mulla' is the name he gave in *Colin Clout's Come Home Again* to the river by his Irish home. But he treats of St. George, of course, not in that poem but *The Faerie Queene*.

> *brogues:* trousers.
> *Ermilin:* archaic form for 'ermine'.

8. *st.*22. *disguised:* in the sense of contorted, unlike itself.

9. *st.*24. *snubs:* sobs.

10. *st.*27. 'VERNON's': Admiral Edward Vernon (1684–1757) became a national hero when in 1739 he redeemed his promise to capture, with only six ships, the Spanish fortress of Porto Bello in the West Indies.

*st.*28. Compare Gray's treatment, in the Elegy, of 'village Hampden' and 'mute inglorious Milton'.

11. *st.*29. 'DENNIS': John Dennis (1657–1734), a by-word for critical severity.

*st.*31. *kesar:* Caesar or Kaiser. cf. Spenser, *The Tears of the Muses:*

> Hir holie things
> Which was the care of Kesars and of Kings.

12. *st.*32. *incondite:* disordered, unformed or ill-formed.

*st.*34. *cakes* . . . SALOPIA's *praises:* Shrewsbury cakes. The circumlocution is deliberately comic.

14. THE VANITY OF HUMAN WISHES 1749

Insofar as Johnson's poem is an imitation, it must be read in the light of what he says, in reference to *The School-Mistress* (see the notes to that poem), on the pleasures to be derived from this kind of poem. Where the poet imitated is a Latin poet, the modern reader, who is normally less conversant with Latin than the readers Johnson first addressed, is deprived of one main source of pleasure in the reading.

T. S. Eliot describes Johnson's poem as '*purer* satire than anything of Dryden or Pope, nearer in spirit to the Latin. For the satirist is in theory a stern moralist castigating the vices of his time or place; and Johnson has a better claim to this seriousness than either Pope or Dryden.' (Mr. Eliot goes on to suggest that in this respect Johnson harks back to the Elizabethan satirists, Marston and Hall, who, though much inferior poets, are 'nearer to the spirit and intention of Juvenal' than Dryden or Pope.)

A reader without Latin can usefully compare Johnson's imitation of the tenth satire of Juvenal with Dryden's translation of the Roman poem. *Juvenal:* Decimus Junius Juvenalis flourished towards the close of the first century. His extant works are sixteen satires, all in heroic hexameters.

SAMUEL JOHNSON, born 1709, son of a Lichfield bookseller, went to Pembroke College, Oxford, with the help of a patron, but was forced by poverty to leave before taking a degree. After an unsuccessful period as a schoolmaster, he came to London in 1737 with his gifted pupil David Garrick; his struggles thereafter as hack-journalist and parliamentary reporter are what lie behind his memorable line, 'Slow rises worth, by poverty depressed'. After *London* in 1738, an imitation of the third satire of Juvenal, he published *The Vanity of Human Wishes* in 1749, having already embarked on his Dictionary of the English Language which occupied him until 1755. Boswell reports of *The Vanity of Human Wishes* that Johnson 'composed seventy lines of it in one day, without putting one of them upon paper until they were finished'. The didactic novel, *Rasselas* (1759), appeared while Johnson was occupied with another great project, his edition of Shakespeare, which appeared in 1765. He also conducted two periodicals, *The Rambler* (1750–2) and *The Idler* (1758–60). Secured from want by a state pension in 1762, it was in 1763 that he met Boswell. His last work was *The Lives of the Poets*. He died in 1784.

*l.*19. *Impeachment stops the speaker's powerful breath.* As Johnson was a Tory, the impeachments that most offended him may well have been those of the Tory ministers, Bolingbroke, Harley, and Ormond in 1715, for their part in concluding the Peace of Utrecht.

15. *l.37-8.* *The needy traveller, serene and gay,*
Walks the wild heath and sings his toil away.

cf. Juvenal, 'Cantabit vacuus coram latrone viator.'

Dryden, 'The beggar sings, ev'n when he sees the place
Beset with thieves, and never mends his pace.'

Chaucer, *Wyf of Bathes Tale—*

'Juvenal seith of poverte myrily:
"The povre man, when he goth by the weye
Bifore the theves he may synge and pleye".'

l.49. *Democritus*, ancient Greek thinker (*c.*460–*c.*370 B.C.), traditionally known as 'the laughing philosopher'.

16. *l.77.* *They mount, they shine, evaporate, and fall.* The image, implicit in the verbs, is of fireworks, harking back by a sort of pun to 'burning to be great'.

l.84. *That hung the bright Palladium of the place.* The portraits of the powerful resident are compared with the statue of Pallas in Troy. Troy could not fall until the Greeks had stolen the image. Romans believed that the true palladium was saved from the Greeks and conveyed by Aeneas to Rome, where it was preserved in the Temple of Vesta.

17. *l.97.* *septennial.* By the Septennial Act of 1716, the duration of each Parliament was extended from three to seven years.

l.99. *Wolsey.* Thomas Wolsey, chief minister of Henry VIII, Archbishop of York and Cardinal, fell from power in 1529 when unable to get Papal approval for the King's divorce of Catherine of Aragon. Johnson treats Wolsey as an instance from English history to correspond to Juvenal's example, Sejanus.

l.127-9. *What gave great Villiers to th'assassin's knife,*
And fix'd disease on Harley's closing life?
What murdered Wentworth, and what exiled Hyde . . .

GEORGE VILLIERS, DUKE OF BUCKINGHAM, favourite of James I, was assassinated by Felton in Portsmouth in 1628. ROBERT HARLEY, EARL OF OXFORD (1661-1724), friend of Swift and Pope, after his impeachment (see note *supra* to *l.*19) was committed to the tower and survived that ordeal seven years. THOMAS WENTWORTH, EARL OF STRAFFORD, minister of Charles I, was impeached by Pym and beheaded in 1641. EDWARD HYDE, EARL OF CLARENDON (1608–74), Charles II's Chancellor, was impeached and died in exile.

18. *l.134. The young enthusiast quits his ease for fame.* In the first half of the eighteenth century 'enthusiast' and 'enthusiasm' were generally terms of contempt. This usage, like others testifying to the Augustans' distrust of emotional excitement without apparent cause, derives from their attitude to the doctrine of 'the inner light' held by the Dissenters of Cromwell's time, whose faith in such ambiguous promptings had (so it seemed to many) plunged England into the anarchy of civil war.

> *l.135–6. Through all his veins the fever of renown*
> *Burns from the strong contagion of the gown;*

cf. Spenser, *Muiopotmos*:

> 'And bowels so with ranckling poyson swelde
> That scarce the skin the strong contagion helde.'

> *l.137–8. O'er Bodley's dome his future labours spread,*
> *And Bacon's mansion trembles o'er his head.*

THOMAS BODLEY restored the University Library, Oxford, which by the middle of the sixteenth century had been completely despoiled. The library was reopened with more than two thousand books in 1602, and in 1617 Bodley, having made further additions, left his property to maintain it.

ROGER BACON, a Franciscan friar, flourished at Oxford, 1214–92, and because of his studies in natural science was reputed to be a wizard.

Johnson's own note on *l.*138 runs as follows: 'There is a tradition that the study of Friar Bacon, built on an arch over the bridge, will fall when a man greater than Bacon shall pass under it. To prevent so shocking an occurrence it was pulled down many years since.'

> *l.155–6. Deign on the passing world to turn thine eyes,*
> *And pause awhile from letters, to be wise;*

cf. Cowley, *Essays*: 'To thy bent Mind some relaxation give
> And steal one day out of thy Life to Live;'
> *ibid:* 'Begin, be bold, and venture to be wise.'

l.158. the patron. Early editions read, 'Toil, envy, want, the garret, and the jail'. Johnson changed 'garret' to 'patron' after his experiences with Chesterfield.

l.159–60. See nations slowly wise, and meanly just,
To buried merit raise the tardy bust.

cf. Ezra Pound (*Guide to Kulchur*, p. 179): 'The "*slowly* wise, and *meanly* just" summarize long observation. They are verse for the man of fifty, who has a right to metrical pleasure perhaps as much as his juniors.'

SAMUEL BUTLER (1612–80), author of *Hudibras*, was given £300 by Charles II, with the promise of more. The promise was never kept and Butler, who died in poverty, was buried at a friend's expense. A monument was raised to him after his death. See Johnson's *Life of Butler*, and protests raised by Oldham and Dryden.

l.162. Hear Lydiat's life, and Galileo's end. THOMAS LYDIAT (1572–1646), a learned divine, was rescued from a debtor's prison by Usher, Laud, and others; he petitioned Charles I without success, suffered for his Royalist sentiments at the hands of the Parliamentarian forces, and died in poverty.

GALILEO, born at Pisa 1564, invented a telescope and as a result of observations made with it he championed the Copernican system of astronomy. Twice brought before the Inquisition because of this and forced to abjure his Copernican beliefs, he died in prison in 1642.

19. *l.166. Rebellion's vengeful talons seize on Laud.* WILLIAM LAUD, Primate of England, pursued a High Church and authoritarian policy in support of Charles I. He was executed in 1643.

l.177–8. Such bribes the rapid Greek o'er Asia whirl'd,
For such the steady Romans shook the world;

F. R. Leavis comments finely (*Revaluation*, p. 118), 'That "steady" turns the vague *cliché*, "shook the world", into the felt percussion of tramping legions'.

19–20. *l.190–220.* 'How just his hopes, let Swedish Charles decide.' Charles XII of Sweden broke up piecemeal the league against him, by defeating the King of Denmark and Peter the Great of Russia, and deposing the King of Poland (*ll.197–8*). Invading Russia, in 1709 he was defeated by Peter the Great at Pultowa (*l.208*). After some years of refuge in the Turkish dominions (*ll.210–12*), he returned to Sweden in 1715, and in 1718 was killed at Fredricshall in Norway, whether by the enemy or by one of his own men is uncertain (*ll.217–8*).

l.200–2–3. 'Think nothing gain'd,' he cries, 'till nought remain,
On Moscow's walls till Gothic standards fly,
And all be mine beneath the polar sky.'

cf. Juvenal: 'Actum, inquit, nihil est, nisi Poeno milite portas
Frangimus, et media vexillum pono Suburra.'

Dryden: 'Yet still uneasie, cries There's nothing done
Till, level with the ground, their gates are laid;
And Punick flags on Roman tow'rs display'd.'

20–21. *l.222–52.* *From Persia's tyrant to Bavaria's lord.* Persia's tyrant, Xerxes (*l.225*), reigned from 485–465 B.C. In 480 he crossed the Hellespont by a bridge of boats, and numbered his combined land and naval forces (*l.227–8*). Herodotus gives the figure as 2,641,610, which is incredible. Though resisted at Thermopylae he entered Athens, but his navy was defeated at Salamis. Fearing for his own safety he went home, leaving an army to be defeated in 479 at Plataea. Bavaria's lord, or 'the bold Bavarian' (*l.239*) was CHARLES ALBERT, ELECTOR OF BAVARIA, who in 1740, when the Austrian Empire passed to Maria Theresa, claimed the Imperial throne (*l.240*), and with the help of the French occupied Vienna (*l.242*). He was elected Emperor. But Maria Theresa ('fair Austria', *l.243*), retiring to Hungary, appealed to her Hungarian subjects ('the wild Hussar' *l.247*), and with British help continued the war of the Austrian Succession. Charles Albert's death in 1745, while the conflict was still undecided, was hastened by the strain of apprehension and insecurity (*l.249–53*).

21. *l.266.* *lenitives:* palliatives (from *lenire*, to assuage).

22. *l.280.* The proximity of 'passions' gives a punning double-meaning to 'will'.

23. *l.311–12.* *From Lydia's monarch should the search descend,*
By Solon caution'd to regard his end, ...

Croesus, last King of Lydia, reigned 560–546 B.C. He asked Solon, the Athenian sage and legislator, who was the happiest man he had ever seen, and received the answer that no man could be called happy until he had made a happy end.

l.315–6. *From Marlb'rough's eyes the streams of dotage flow,*
And Swift expires a driv'ler and a show.'

The Duke of Marlborough, the great commander, in the last years of his life partially lost the use of his faculties, from the shock of losing first a son and then a daughter.

From 1736 until his death in 1745, Swift suffered from fits, which at first brought on mania and towards the end reduced him to a state of idiocy.

l.319–20.   *Yet Vane could tell what ills from beauty spring;*
               And Sedley curs'd the form that pleas'd a King.

Anne Vane, mistress of Frederick Prince of Wales, died in 1736. Caroline Sedley was the mistress of James II.

ELEGY WRITTEN IN A COUNTRY CHURCHYARD   1750

Johnson writes, in his *Life of Gray*, 'In the character of his *Elegy* I rejoice to concur with the common reader; for by the common sense of readers uncorrupted with literary prejudices, after all the refinement of subtilty and the dogmatism of learning, must be finally decided all claim to poetical honours. The *Church-yard* abounds with images which find a mirror in every mind, and with sentiments to which every bosom returns an echo.'

Gray's attitude to those who applauded this poem while objecting to all the others of Gray, may be gathered from what is reported of him by a contemporary: '. . . his "Churchyard Elegy", which, he told me, with a good deal of acrimony, owed its popularity entirely to the subject, and that the public would have received it as well if it had been written in prose.'

It has long been known that the composition of the Elegy occupied Gray, off and on, from 1742 to 1748 or 1749. Recent study by H. W. Garrod enables us to date the writing more exactly. See note to *st*.18.

THOMAS GRAY, born in London in 1716, studied at Peterhouse, Cambridge, where he was later elected to a fellowship. He spent the remainder of his life resentfully at Cambridge, except for travels to the continent with Horace Walpole (1740–1), to Scotland (1765), and to the Lake District (1769). His impressions of these journeys, in his letters, make up the first full manifestation of the Romantic attitude to natural landscape. Appointed Professor of History in 1768, he died in 1771.

25.   *st*.1.   At a time when the exclamatory style of Young's *Night Thoughts* was greatly fashionable, it was seriously suggested that the first line be altered to read: 'The curfew tolls! The knell of parting day!' Gray himself indicated a source for the line, in Dante.

26.   *st*.6.   cf. Thomson, *Winter*:

               'In vain for him the officious wife prepares
               The fire fair-blazing and the vestments warm;
               In vain his little children, peeping out
               Into the mingling storm, demand their sire . . .'

and Collins, *Popular Superstitions of the Highlands*:

> 'For him, in vain, the anxious wife shall wait
>   Or wander forth to meet him on his way;
> For him, in vain, at to-fall of the day
> His babes shall linger at the unclosing gate . . .'

but also Lucretius:

> 'Jam jam non domus accipiet te lacta, neque uxor
>   Optima, nec dulces occurrent oscula nati
> Praeripere . . .'
>   (See J. M. Murry, *Countries of the Mind*).

27. *st.*14. 'Full many a flower is born to blush unseen,
           And waste its sweetness on the desert air.'

See William Empson (*Some Versions of Pastoral*): 'a gem does not mind being in a cave and a flower prefers not to be picked; we feel that the man is like the flower, as short-lived, natural and valuable, and this tricks us into feeling that he is better off without opportunities.'

28. *st.*18. A MS preserved in Eton College here departs from the accepted text, and concludes the poem with four more stanzas:

> The thoughtless World to Majesty may bow
> Exalt the brave, & idolize Success
> But more to Innocence their Safety owe
> Than Power & Genius e'er conspired to bless.
>
> And thou, who mindful of the unhonour'd Dead
> Dost in these Notes their artless Tale relate
> By Night & lonely Contemplation led
> To linger in the gloomy Walks of Fate,
>
> Hark how the sacred Calm that broods around
> Bids ev'ry fierce tumultuous Passion cease
> In still small Accents whisp'ring from the Ground
> A grateful Earnest of eternal Peace.
>
> No more with Reason & thyself at Strife
> Give anxious Cares & endless Wishes room
> But thro' the cool sequester'd Vale of Life
> Pursue the silent Tenour of thy Doom.

Professor Garrod (in *Essays presented to David Nichol Smith*) has established that this was the poem as it stood complete after Gray had worked on it in 1742; all that follows was written in 1746–7. F. W. Bateson (in *English Poetry. A Critical Introduction*) has suggested that Gray revised the 1742 version because it was too personal for publication, being written under the stress of his quarrel with Horace Walpole, which led the poet to dwell upon inequalities of status and opportunity (as in *sts*.16 and 17), such inequalities as divided himself, newly impoverished by his father's death in 1741, from his erstwhile friend, Walpole, son of a rich and powerful politician. By 1746 Walpole and Gray were friends again, and (so Mr. Bateson suggests) the latter then extended and worked over the poem to remove from it traces of his own resentment, so blunting the edge of its social criticism.

st.19   Note Gray's adaptation of an idea from the cancelled stanzas in the Eton College MS.

28–29. *st*.20–23.   Johnson remarks: 'The four stanzas beginning *Yet even these bones,* are to me original: I have never seen the notions in any other place; yet he that reads them here, persuades himself that he has always felt them. Had Gray written often thus, it had been vain to blame, and useless to praise him.'

29. *st*.24.   *For thee:* Is 'thee' the cutter of epitaphs, or the 'me' of *l*.4?

30. *st*.30–32.   Landor spoke of 'the tin-kettle of an epitaph tied to its tail'. Its subject is the ambiguous 'thee' of *st*.24.

31. A SONG TO DAVID   1763

See on the structure of Smart's poem, R. D. Havens in the *Review of English Studies,* Vol. 14 (April 1938), pp. 178–82. The stanzas are elaborately grouped 'in threes, or sevens or their multiples—the mystic numbers'. For instance after three stanzas of invocation come two groups of seven describing David, then three sets of three describing the themes of David's singing, and a further set of three describing the effects of his singing. And so on: see the notes for further indications of Professor Havens' argument. This structure is partly brought out, but in part also obscured, by Smart's own prefatory 'Argument'.

CHRISTOPHER SMART, born in Kent in 1722, spent his boyhood in Durham under the protection of the ancient and powerful Barnard family of Raby Castle. It has been suggested that a dominant influence throughout his life was a youthful love for Anne Vane, of the Barnard family. Assisted still by the same patrons, Smart went up to Cambridge where he distinguished himself as a scholar and (already) as poet. Elected fellow of Pembroke in 1745, notoriously riotous and improvident, he left Cambridge about 1749 to maintain himself as a freelance journalist in London. Married in 1753, he appears to have been confined for insanity from 1756 to 1763. After his release ensued a period of hard work and relatively orderly life, but despite a pension secured for him he was soon in want again, and in 1769 he was in prison for debt. He died in 1771.

Johnson's view of Smart the man, as reported by Boswell, is too good to miss: 'I did not think he ought to be shut up. His infirmities were not noxious to society. He insisted on people praying with him; and I'd as lief pray with Kit Smart as anyone else. Another charge was that he did not love clean linen; and I have no passion for it.'

32. *st*.4 Note the twelve epithets in the first three lines. Each of these is expanded in turn in the next twelve stanzas, which with this stanza and another to close the sequence, accordingly make up a group of twice seven.

33. *st*.6. *the boaster:* Goliath.
    st.8. *En-gedi:* I Samuel xxiv.
    st.9. *play:* 'ply'.

34. *st*.10. *sublime:* The ancient treatise known ever since the Renaissance as *Longinus on the Sublime,* came into its own with English readers and writers when Addison commended it. Edmund Burke's essay on *The Sublime and the Beautiful* (1756) is only the most elaborate of many analyses of the sublime. By the end of the century 'the sublime' (in literature but also in other arts and in natural landscape) was distinguished not only from the beautiful but also from the picturesque. Smart may well have in mind especially Robert Lowth's Oxford lectures on Hebrew poetry, which Lowth found pre-eminently 'sublime'.
    st.12. *Kidron:* 2 Samuel xv.

35. *st*.14. *Ziba and Mephibosheth:* 2 Samuel xvi and xix.
    st.15. *ephod:* a priestly garment, see 2 Samuel vi.

*st.*17.   *Michal, Abishag:* two of David's wives, one the wife of his youth, the other of his age.

36.   *st.*18.   This starts a new group, of three times three, naming David's themes.

*st.*19.   *citterns:* harps.

39.   *st.*30.   *The pillars of the Lord are seven.* It is suspected that in this stanza, as in the seven which follow where each of the pillars is given a letter of the Greek alphabet, Smart is using the secret symbolism of Freemasonry. But cf. *The Monthly Review* (April 1763). Note that stanzas 30 to 37, together with 38 which clearly looks back over the sequence as an epilogue, make up another group of 3×3.

40.   *st.*35.   *chapitre:* the capital or head-stone of a column.

*st.*37.   *And closed th' infernal draught.* Unintentionally comic and all the more delightful, this line seems to mean that by rearing the last of the seven pillars the Creator completed the edifice, and so, as if with a door, shut out the winds of Hell which sought to shake it down.

41.   *st.*38.   'symbol' and 'type' are here precisely distinguished, and 'type' carries a specially precise, even pedantic, meaning.

*st.*40.   This inaugurates a new sequence, based on the Ten Commandments freely varied and expanded, which lasts to *st.*48—another group of 9.

42.   *st.*42.   *wilk:* whelk. cf. *Jubilate Agno:* 'Let Jona rejoice with the Wilk—Wilks, Wilkie, and Wilkinson bless the name of the Lord Jesus.'

43.   *st.*44.   It will be observed that Smart's morality is unorthodox. 'With fear concupiscence to curb' loses its force in view of 'rapture to transport', which follows, and the admonition 'Use all thy passions!'.

*st.*48.   *Grutch not:* grudge not.

Note the vividness of colloquial usage: 'Work emulation up . . .'

44.   *st.*50.   This introduces the most elaborate of all the stanza groups, turning upon the crucial phrase 'For Adoration', in the first line of *sts.*51 and 52, in the second of 53, the third of 54, and so on to 57; then in the first line of 58, the second of 59, and so on to 63; thereafter in the first line of every stanza up to 71. Smart appears to want to maintain a

sevenfold arrangement; he does so, since his is a six-line stanza, by giving in each case (51 and 52; 64 and 65) two stanzas in which 'For Adoration' figures in the first line, before it begins to slip down through the six lines of the stanza.

st.52. *cheques:* chequers. Note the three verbs 'Adjust, attract, and fill', anticipating the effect at the close of the poem. Seasonal change throughout the year is traced through succeeding stanzas up to the wintry scenes of 62 and 63.

st.53. *Ivis:* humming bird.

45. st.55. *The spotted ounce:* leopard.
For ADORATION *beasts embark:* cf. *The Monthly Review*, 1763. 'We remember to have somewhere read of a certain quadruped which puts to sea on a piece of timber, in order to prey on fish. But we have no account of such embarkation in any natural Historian of credit . . .' cf. Smart's footnote to this effect in edition of 1765.

> '*While waves upholding halcyon's ark*
> *No longer roar and toss.*'

It was believed in antiquity and for long afterwards, that the halcyon or kingfisher nested on the surface of the sea, and that perfect calm ('halcyon weather') coincided with the bird's breeding season.

st.57. *crusions:* carp.

46. st.60. *thyine:* sweet.

47. st.62. Poetic diction was never more curious and elaborate than in the phrases found by Smart for the freezing of water ('Where frosts the waves condense'), and the protective coloration of the ermine's winter-fur.

st.64. *translation:* a Latinate usage, meaning the transference of the soul from terrestrial life to eternal.

48. st.66. *The Lord's philosopher:* i.e. the natural philosopher, or scientist. But cf. Smart's source, Delany's *Life and Reign of David*.

st.68. *bezoar:* a substance abstracted from the stomachs of some animals; *Galbanum:* gum-resin, used in incense.

st.69. *anana:* a kind of pineapple.

49. st.72. Here begins the last group of stanzas, again arranged by threes: 72 to 74, 'Sweet', 'Sweet', and 'Sweeter'; 75 to 77, 'Strong',

'Strong', and 'Stronger'; 78 to 80, 'Beauteous', 'Beauteous', and 'beauteous more'; 81 to 83, 'Precious', 'Precious', and 'more precious'; 84 to 86, 'Glorious', 'Glorious', and 'more glorious'.

50. *st.75.* *glede:* hawk; *xiphias:* sword-fish.

51. *st.78.* *meditated wild:* an ornate locution for nature's wildness trimmed into premeditated patterns by the gardener.

st.81. *alba:* the alb or surplice.

54. THE DESERTED VILLAGE   1770

The eighteenth-century poets are in our day often criticized for planning a poem just as they planned an essay, a treatise or a survey; so that the structure of their poems follows the rules of discursive logic rather than a logic of the imagination. This objection must in great measure be admitted. Yet *The Deserted Village* is an example of poems consciously planned like essays, which yet appeal through a hidden imaginative continuity. Throughout, from the very second couplet where a floating petal comes to rest, Goldsmith associates rural life with images of fragility like the life of a flower, the bloom on the skin of fruit, trembling and shrinking and flying, murmurs on the wind, a guttering candle, a hunted hare. The natural, which we think of as robust, is thus associated with what is vulnerable and fugitive. Another poet might have presented this as the paradox which it is. Though Goldsmith chooses not to point it up in this way, the paradox is present and pervasive; and expressed in the mutually assisting emotional reverberations of words whose logical connection is slight, it gives the poem a truly poetic unity beyond the reach of the prose essay.

OLIVER GOLDSMITH, born in 1728, the fifth son of a country rector at Pallas, Co. Longford, was educated at Trinity College, Dublin, where he was undisciplined and largely unsuccessful. After trying in vain to enter the clerical and legal professions, he studied medicine at Edinburgh, Leyden, and Louvain, and after wanderings on the Continent, settled in London in 1756. Several years followed in which he eked out a living by hack-journalism on the one hand and on the other by intermittent practice as a physician. About 1759 his fortunes began to improve as he devoted more of his time to literature, and in 1761 he met Johnson. *The Traveller* appeared in 1764, *The Vicar of Wakefield* in 1766. His comedy, *The Good Natur'd Man*, was produced in 1768, and was followed in 1773 by *She Stoops to Conquer*. Improvident and needy to the last, Goldsmith died in 1774.

l.1. *Auburn.* The name is fictitious, and there has been much discussion how far Goldsmith painted an English village, how far an Irish one. It is not disputed that the features of the description correspond to those of Lissoy, the Irish village where Goldsmith spent his boyhood, nor that the ejection of the villagers took place, as in the poem, when the landlord of Lissoy extended his private estate. On the other hand one cannot believe with Macaulay that the English source for the poem is limited to the description of the village while still prosperous; similar calamities, though they may have stopped short of wholesale depopulation, overtook English villages as well as Irish ones, in Goldsmith's day.

55. *l*.27. *The swain mistrustless of his smutted face*—the rustic is the victim of a practical joke: soot has been smeared on his face without his knowing it.

l.42. *But choked with sedges works its weedy way*—note the felicity of 'works'.

58. *l*.155. The demobilised soldier reduced to beggary figures in *The Country Justice* and in more than one early poem by Wordsworth. And Cowper in *The Task* similarly protests at the scandal.

59. *l*.189–92. Lucan, Statius, and Claudian from Latin literature, also French poems by Chapelain and the Abbé de Chaulieu, have been cited as sources for this simile. It is anticipated in English by Young in *Night Thoughts*:

'As some tall Tow'r, or lofty Mountain's Brow,
Detains the Sun, Illustrious from its Height,
While rising Vapours, and descending Shades,
With Damps and Darkness drown the Spatious Vale:
Undampt by Doubt, Undarken'd by Despair,
Philander, thus, augustly rears his Head.'

60. *l*.232. *The twelve good rules, the royal game of goose.* Crabbe in *The Parish Register* similarly alludes to an old broadside, 'King Charles' Twelve Good Rules', which listed twelve homely maxims under a woodcut of the execution of Charles I. The game of goose was played by moving along a board by the throw of dice, as in 'Snakes and Ladders'.

62.   *l.298.   Its vistas strike, its palaces surprise.* The vocabulary of the landscape gardener—his 'striking vistas' and 'surprise views'—is here used with bitter irony. 'Strike' for instance is almost a pun: the vista strikes as a plague or epidemic strikes.

  l.299.   the smiling land. Note how the stock epithet 'smiling' is given a new tragic implication: the land smiles heartlessly on the wretched.

64.   *l.344.   wild Altama:* the River Alatamaha in Georgia. The first ill-fated attempt to settle this region was made in 1732 under the leadership of General Oglethorpe, friend of Goldsmith and Johnson.

65.   *l.389–94.* Goldsmith here re-animates the dead, or in his time dying, metaphor of the state as 'the body politic'.

66.   *l.418.   On Torno's cliffs, or Pambamarca's side.* The River Tornea, flowing between Sweden and Finland; Pambamarca is a mountain near Quito in South America.

  l.427–30. These last four lines are by Johnson.

66.   RETALIATION   1774

  This poem was written in the last months of Goldsmith's life, and left unfinished. The circumstances in which it was composed are given in an unsigned letter to the publisher, which prefaced the poem on its first appearance: 'Dr. Goldsmith belonged to a Club of Beaux Esprits, where Wit sparkled sometimes at the Expence of Good-nature. It was proposed to write Epitaphs on the Doctor; his Country, Dialect and Person, furnished Subjects of Witticism.—The Doctor was called on for Retaliation, and at their next Meeting produced the following Poem. . . .' Cumberland, Garrick, and others have left slightly different accounts of the occasion. Of the extempore epitaphs to which Goldsmith retaliated, the only one to survive is Garrick's:

> 'Here lies Nolly Goldsmith, for shortness call'd Noll,
> Who wrote like an angel, but talk'd like poor Poll.'

(Goldsmith was notoriously a poor conversationalist—quite the least Irish thing about him.) It should be noted that the gathering was not of the famous 'Literary Club', where Johnson presided, but was at the St. James's coffee-house, erstwhile the haunt of Addison and Swift.

l.1.　*Scarron:* Paul Scarron (1610–60). Goldsmith's translation of Scarron's *Roman Comique* appeared in 1776.

l.5.　*Our Dean:* Dr. Thomas Barnard, Dean of Derry, died in 1806.

l.6.　*Our Burke:* Edmund Burke, 1729–97.

l.7.　*Our Will:* William Burke, a relative of Edmund and M.P., died in 1798.

l.8.　*And Dick:* Richard Burke, Edmund's brother, on leave from the West Indies, where he was Collector to the Customs at Grenada.

l.9.　*Our Cumberland:* Richard Cumberland, playwright, 1732–1811.

l.10.　*Douglas:* Dr. Douglas, later Bishop of Salisbury, died in 1807.

67.　*l*.14.　*Ridge:* John Ridge, an Irish barrister.
　　　　　　Reynolds: Sir Joshua Reynolds the painter, 1723–92.

l.15.　*Hickey:* Thomas Hickey, another Irish lawyer, died in 1794.

l.34.　*Tommy Townshend:* M.P., later Lord Sydney, died in 1803. Boswell says Goldsmith introduced his name to pay him out for having in Parliament opposed the granting of a pension to Johnson.

l.36.　*And thought of convincing, while they thought of dining—* Burke's oratory was so little to the taste of the House of Commons that he was nicknamed 'the Dinner Bell'.

68.　*l*.54.　*Now breaking a jest, and now breaking a limb.* See note to 2nd ed., on Richard Burke—'The above Gentleman having slightly fractured one of his arms and legs, at different times, the doctor has rallied him on those accidents, as a kind of *retributive* justice for breaking his jests on other people.'

l.62.　*The Terence of England:* Terence, Latin comic playwright (195–159 B.C.).

l.65–6.　'*His gallants are all faultless, his women divine,*
　　　　　　And comedy wonders at being so fine;'
Cumberland wrote sentimental comedies, a *genre* which Goldsmith attacked in his preface to *The Good Natur'd Man*. Both of Goldsmith's plays are written to replace sentimental elevation in comedy by robustness and realism.

68–69.　*l*.79–92.　Douglas exposed the pretensions of William Lauder, who criticized Milton, and Archibald Bower, author of *A History of the Popes* (see *l*.89), both Scots, as Douglas was. *Our Dodds* (*l*.86) refers to the Revd. Dr. William Dodd, who in 1777 was executed for forgery; *our Kenricks* (same line) refers to Dr. Kenrick, a journalist who had attacked Goldsmith, and in 1774 was giving public lectures on Shakespeare.

69. *l.*115. *Ye Kenricks, ye Kellys, and Woodfalls so grave*—Hugh Kelly (1739–77), an Irish writer of sentimental comedies such as *False Delicacy*, 1768. William Woodfall was a theatrical critic.

70. *l.*120. *To act as an angel*—note the neat double-meaning.

*l.*146. *He shifted his trumpet, and only took snuff.* Reynolds was deaf and used an ear-trumpet, as in one of his self-portraits.

In the fifth edition the poem concluded with twenty-eight further lines on Caleb Whitefoord, a Scottish wine-merchant, wit, and connoisseur. As the authenticity of these is disputed, they are here omitted.

71. THE COUNTRY JUSTICE, PART I   1774

The poem on its first appearance was described as 'By one of his Majesty's Justices of the Peace for the County of Somerset'; and was prefaced by a letter of dedication, 'To Richard Burn, LL.D., one of his Majesty's Justices of the Peace for the Counties of Westmorland and Cumberland'. Dr. Burn, who was the author of a digest of the laws concerning Justices of the Peace (1754), is thought to have suggested the poem to Langhorne, and to have provided the poet with information.

Wordsworth wrote of *The Country Justice*, in a letter of 15th January 1837, 'As far as I know it is the first Poem, unless perhaps Shenstone's School-Mistress be excepted, that fairly brought the Muse into the Company of Common Life, to which it comes nearer than Goldsmith, and upon which it looks with a tender and enlightened humanity—and with a charitable (and being so), philosophical and poetical construction that is too rarely found in the works of Crabbe. It is not without many faults in style from which Crabbe's more austere judgment preserved him—but these are to me trifles in a work so original and touching.'

JOHN LANGHORNE, born in Westmorland in 1735, was educated at Appleby and went as tutor to a family at Ripon. After a period teaching at Wakefield, and as tutor to the Cracroft family in Lincolnshire, he obtained in 1761 a curacy at Dagenham. His first poems had already appeared; now followed a novel, *Solyman and Almena*. Appointed to a London parish in 1764, he married Anne Cracroft whom he had courted for years, but she died in childbirth. While in London Langhorne entered into controversy with Charles Churchill, and in 1765 edited the poems of Collins. In 1767 he moved to a living in Somerset, but thereafter spent much time at Folkestone where he collaborated with his brother William, also a clergyman, on a translation of Plutarch which appeared in 1770. Returning to Somerset, he was appointed J.P., and this inspired *The Country Justice*. Having lost a second wife, Langhorne died in 1779.

*l.*1–6. The reference is to Robin Hood.

71–72. *l.*21–24. *Paoli.*˙ Many Corsican insurrections against Genoese rule had gone unnoticed. All of Europe felt an interest in the Corsican rebels in the 1760s, partly because of the general enthusiasm for a 'state of nature', which the Corsicans, turbulent and hardy, were thought to exemplify; and partly because the Corsican leader PASQUALE PAOLI (1726–1807) was supposed privy in 1764 to Buttafoco's inviting Rousseau, philosophical patentee of 'the state of nature', to draft a constitution for the island. Paoli's most influential champion in Britain was James Boswell, who visited Corsica in 1765, published an account of it in 1768, collected money for the Corsican cause, and wore Corsican national dress on conspicuous occasions. Boswell failed in his attempt to secure British intervention, and in 1769 Corsica was ceded to France. (Hence Napoleon Bonaparte was to be born a French citizen.) Paoli sought refuge in England. Langhorne's reference is to Corsicans who supposedly continued to resist both French and Genoese; to such diehards Paoli's departure would have looked like treachery.

72. *l.*32. *The far-fam'd Edward.* Edward III, here celebrated as having instituted the office of J.P.

*l.*57. *Harewood.* Langhorne may be supposed here to recall the period of his youthful stay in Ripon. Harewood House is near by.

73. *l.*62, 65, 72. *cits.* A contemptuous abbreviation for 'citizen'. The repetition, deliberately contrived to express mounting annoyance, is in effect very awkward and insipid.

*l.*73–78. *Ye royal architects, whose antic taste . . .*—here, and again (much more finely) in *l.*113–16, Langhorne mocks the planning of Kew Gardens by Sir William Chambers, who in his 'Dissertation on Oriental Gardening' (1772) had envisaged a 'Chinese garden' where 'bats, owls, vultures, and every bird of prey flutter in the groves; wolves, tigers and jackalls howl in the forests; . . .' etc.

l.92. *surbase:* 'a border or moulding immediately above the base or lower panelling of a wainscoted room.' (O.E.D.)

74. *l.104.* *traditionary:* traditional.

75. *l.140.* *Born but to err, and erring to bewail*—cf. Pope, 'Essay on Man'. 'Born to die, and reas'ning but to err;'

l.156. *Folly's Misfortune in the first Degree*—this fine line deserves to be proverbial.

75–76. *l.161–6.* *Cold on Canadian Hills, or Minden's Plain*—These were the lines which drew approval from Burns, when quoted by Sir Walter Scott on the only occasion on which they met.

l.183–4. *Not Wilkes, our Freedom's holy Martyr, more;*
Nor his firm Phalanx of the common Shore.

JOHN WILKES (1727–1797), son of a magnate of the City of London, was conspicuous as pamphleteer and debauchee as well as politician. He successfully resisted government and court in the interests of freedom of journalistic comment. Langhorne, as a supporter of the Court interest and an opponent of the Whigs, had earlier crossed swords with Wilkes's poetic champion, Churchill. 'Freedom's holy Martyr' is sarcastic, as appears when Langhorne sees support for Wilkes as emanating from 'the common Shore', i.e. the open sewer.

77. *l.204.* *Marian, whom Gay in sweetest Strains has sung!* See 'Tuesday, or the Ditty', from *The Shepherd's Week* (1714) by John Gay, 1685–1732.

80. THE COUNTRY JUSTICE, PART II   1775

The dedicatory stanzas are addressed to a member of the Cracroft family to whom Langhorne went as tutor in 1759. Their home was at Hackthorn, near Lincoln (see *st.*6), but the reference to Essex in *st.*5 must allude to a period after 1761, when Langhorne went to Dagenham. He kept in touch with the Cracrofts after leaving their services, as he was paying his addresses to the daughter of the family.

*l.*7. In an early edition a note to this line runs: 'The Mahometan princes seem to have a regular system of begging. Nothing so common as to hear that the Dey of Algiers, etc. etc. are dissatisfied with their presents. It must be owned, it would be for the welfare of the world, if princes in general would adhere to the maxim, that *it is better to beg than to steal.*'

l.24. *Teniers.* Of the Flemish family of Teniers, talented as painters through several generations, the one probably intended here is David Teniers the younger, 1610–94, famous for his paintings of scenes from peasant life.

84. *l.152.* *Brighthelmstone.* i.e. Brighton, at this date, just entering upon its reputation as a fashionable watering-place.

l.163. *Blood! Maccorone! Cicisbeo! or Rook!* These are the titles sought at various periods by young men about town who aspired to be thought 'fast'.

85. *l.166–7.* *From BERTIE's, ALMACK's, ARTHUR's, and the Nest*
    Where JUDAH's ferrets earth with CHARLES unblest;—

The names in the first line are those of fashionable London clubs. In view of a passage in Part III, it appears that *Charles unblest* is Charles James Fox, 1749–1806, at this time just starting his brilliant political career but already notorious for being, because of his love of gambling, in the hands of Jewish money-lenders.

l.184. *LINLEY's voice.* Elizabeth Ann Linley (1754–92), a famous singer and beauty, eloped in 1772 with the playwright Richard Brinsley Sheridan, whom she married in 1773.

87. *l.243.* *His creeping soul in Sternhold's creeping lays*—Thomas Sternhold who died in 1549 collaborated with John Hopkins (d. 1570), in versifying the psalms.

88. THE COUNTRY JUSTICE PART III   1777

l.1. *Sir John.* Sir John Fielding, famous magistrate and brother of Henry Fielding the novelist, died in 1780.

l.3. *Gay's brave robber.* Captain MacHeath in Gay's *The Beggar's Opera.*

l.17. *Together let us beat all Giles's Fields.* The parish of St. Giles-in-the-Fields was throughout the eighteenth century the most notorious of London's Irish quarters, a byword for vice, poverty and disease.

l.24. *But stop and call at Stephen's in their Way.* By 'Stephen's', Langhorne means the House of Commons, so called from its old meeting-place in St. Stephen's Chapel of the old Palace of Westminster. As a staunch supporter of Lord North, Langhorne here enters into political controversy.

89. *l.31-2.* *Good Lord, Sir John, how would the People stare*
To see the present and the late Lord Mayor

A note in early editions advises the reader that this was written in 1776. Thus the two Lord Mayors intended are John Wilkes, holding the office 1774-5, and John Sawbridge, who succeeded him. The point is that both were also M.P.s and Whigs, bitterly opposed to the government of Lord North.

l.45-7. *When with black Wing she swept the Western Main!* In this and the succeeding lines Langhorne rebukes the American colonists for breaking loose from the Mother country.

l.54. *Ch-m.* William Pitt the elder, Earl of Chatham.

l.61. *From Charles quite graceless, up to Grafton's Grace!* cf. Part II, *l.167.* Charles James Fox, like the Duke of Grafton, opposed the government's attempt to coerce the colonists.

l.62. *Forty-five.* No. 45. of Wilkes' *North Briton* was crucial.
90. *l.65.* *And Wilkes and Humphrey number'd with the Dead*—Humphrey Cotes, a close friend of Wilkes, and Churchill's executor, had died in 1775.

l.75. *When the gilt Nabob lacqueys all the Way:* cf. Pope, *Elegy to the Memory of an Unfortunate Lady,* 'While the long fun'rals blacken all the way'. For 'Nabob' see the Introduction.

l.80-1. *Are these mock Ruins that invade my View?*
These are the Entrails of the poor Gentoo.

The magnate of the East India Company, retiring to England, adorns his estate according to a new fad with specially constructed 'picturesque' ruins, paying for this out of a fortune accumulated by exploiting the Indians. 'Gentoo' is a corruption of the Portuguese 'gentio', a Gentile or heathen, applied by the Portuguese to the Hindu, to distinguish him from the 'moro', or moor, the moslem.

91. *l.114.* *The savage Law.* Early editions note it as 7Jac.C.4, an enactment of the time of James I, who accordingly, in *l.118-25* is subjected to a piece of splendid invective. This law ordained that a woman bearing an illegitimate child could be sent to prison for it.

93. YARDLEY-OAK   1791
This poem was discovered among Cowper's papers after his death by his first biographer William Hayley, who published it in his *Life*

and Posthumous Writings of William Cowper, Esqr. (new and enlarged edition, 1806). Hayley decides, 'It must have been written in the year 1791; and, as other poetical pursuits, particularly his translations from Milton, engrossed his attention in the course of that year, I apprehend he threw this admirable fragment aside, and absolutely forgot it'. In these circumstances, and since the piece is unfinished, it is important to note Hayley's further observation, 'I never saw any of his compositions more carefully, or more judiciously, corrected'. The poem was a favourite of Wordsworth's who, on its first appearance, copied it into his commonplace book.

Yardley Oak stood in Yardley Chase, an estate of the Earls of Northampton, about five miles from Cowper's home at Weston-Underwood.

WILLIAM COWPER was born in 1731. His father was a country rector but the family was ancient and eminent; through his mother, who died when the poet was six, he claimed descent from John Donne. Educated at Westminster School, Cowper was trained for the law; but on the brink of securing by family influence a position in the Houses of Parliament, Cowper's congenital hypochondria was aggravated by separation from the cousin he intended to marry, and by the death of his father and of a close friend. He suffered from delusions, and attempted suicide. After a period in a mental asylum in 1763, Cowper slowly recovered and moved to Huntingdon where he entered the household of the Unwins. Mr. Unwin died soon afterwards, and Cowper and the widow moved to Olney in Bucks, at the instigation of the famous evangelical clergyman, John Newton, with whom Cowper collaborated on the Olney hymns. Cowper's first collection of poems, in 1782, was unsuccessful. But *The Task*, published with other poems in 1785, brought him fame. He moved his home the two miles from Olney to Weston-Underwood, still with Mrs. Unwin, who nursed him devotedly through recurrent fits of insanity perhaps aggravated by evangelical Calvinism. Cowper published his translation of Homer in 1791. After the death of Mrs. Unwin he enjoyed only short intervals of lucidity until his own death in 1800. His posthumously published Letters are often esteemed as highly as his poems.

l.5. and with excoriate forks deform. 'Deform', used as a participle instead of 'deformed', follows Latin usage rather than English. Such usages, together with frequent inversions and polysyllabic learned words like 'excoriate', are modelled upon the Latinate diction of the

Miltonic epic. Cowper was preparing an edition of Milton at the time of writing this poem.

93–96. *l.*23–26. In the fourth foot of *l.*24 ('mellow'd'), and the third foot of *l.*26 ('dibbling'), Cowper asks for a stress on the first syllable rather than on the second, thus checking and roughening the iambic run. Cowper in his *Table Talk* demanded, as the modern ear demands, more such metrical variation than Cowper's age, with its esteem for 'smoothness' in versification and for the 'correctness' of Pope, was in general prepared to allow. A still more striking example is *l.*46—'The clock of history, facts and events . . .'.

*l.*35. *as theirs the fabled Twins*—Castor and Pollux, twin legendary heroes placed among the stars as the constellation *Gemini*, in one version of the myth, sprang from the egg laid by Leda after Zeus had visited her in the form of a swan.

*l.*41. *Dodona*, the most ancient oracle of Greece, speaking through a grove of oak-trees. The sound of the wind through the trees, accentuated by brazen vessels hung on the boughs, was regarded as the voice of the god, its message elucidated by priests or, later, priestesses.

96. *l.*99. *knee-timber*. Hayley observes: 'Knee-Timber is found in the crooked arms of oak, which by reason of their distortion, are easily adjusted to the angle formed where the deck and the ship's sides meet.'

*l.*116. *Yet is thy root sincere*. There is a pun on the basic meaning. of 'sincerus' in Latin (unspoiled, sound, and whole) and 'sincere' in English.

97. *l.*126. *rovers of the forest wild*, i.e. charcoal-burners.

99. THE OLD CUMBERLAND BEGGAR   1797–8

Written in 1797–8, *The Old Cumberland Beggar* appeared in the second edition of *Lyrical Ballads*, published in 1800. It is, of course, neither 'lyrical' nor 'a ballad', even in the special meanings Wordsworth gave to both those words. See H. V. D. Dyson, ' "The Old Cumberland Beggar" and the Wordsworthian Unities', in 'Essays on the Eighteenth Century presented to D. Nichol Smith'; and particularly Mr. Dyson's remarks on 'the community of man with his fellows' as the main subject of the poem—'In all except the very earliest stages of Wordsworth's life this is really more important to him than unity with his physical environment. The quality of his dealings with nature was highly exceptional, perhaps unique; in his relationships with himself and his fellow

128

men he was deeply sensible of needs shared, though not always understood, by everyone.'

The subject was topical, as Wordsworth in later life remarked, when he dictated a note on the poem: 'The political economists were about that time beginning their war upon mendicity in all its forms, and by implication, if not directly, on alms-giving also.'

WILLIAM WORDSWORTH, born in 1770, studied in Cambridge. After a period in France, Wordsworth returned to England with a mind divided between English patriotism and sympathy with the French Revolution; his distress was accentuated by his having abandoned a Frenchwoman by whom he had had a child. Saved by the devotion of his sister, Dorothy, a bequest from a patron, and friendship with Coleridge, Wordsworth recovered his composure in Somerset where he now settled, and collaborated with Coleridge on 'Lyrical Ballads' (1798–1800). Introduced by Coleridge to German idealist philosophy, Wordsworth tried over many years to comply with his friend's request for a philosophical poem, but of this project all that remains is the massive rambling narrative, 'The Excursion', published in 1714; and the no less massive autobiographical 'Prelude'. Wordsworth married in 1802, and his poems thereafter became more sedulously perfect in form, but less realistic, and incorporated less criticism of society. Created laureate in 1843, he lived on till 1850, but his most memorable work was produced before 1810.

104. *l.179*. *'May never* HOUSE, *misnamed of* INDUSTRY'—See Wordsworth's letter to Charles James Fox of 1801, accompanying the volumes in which this poem first appeared, together with others on related themes such as *Michael* and *The Brothers*:

'But recently by the spreading of manufactures through every part of the country, by the heavy taxes upon postage, by workhouses, Houses of Industry, and the invention of Soup-shops, &c. &c. superadded to the encreasing disproportion between the price of labour and that of the necessaries of life, the bonds of domestic feeling among the poor, as far as the influence of these things has extended, have been weakened, and in innumerable instances entirely destroyed. The evil would be the less to be regretted, if these institutions were regarded only as palliatives to a disease; but the vanity and pride of their promoters are so subtly interwoven with them, that they are deemed great discoveries and blessings to humanity.'

Wordsworth's dislike of professional 'do-gooders', expressed here and by implication in his poem, together with his opposition to all forms of institutionalized regimentation in favour of communal usage and unwritten law, is a striking example of the innate conservatism of a man who a few years before had been under suspicion by the authorities for his sympathy with revolutionary France.